Central Asia in World History

The
New
Oxford
World
History

Central Asia in World History

Peter B. Golden

UNIVERSITY PRESS

2011

OXFORD
UNIVERSITY PRESS

Oxford University Press, Inc., publishes works that further
Oxford University's objective of excellence
in research, scholarship, and education.

Oxford   New York
Auckland   Cape Town   Dar es Salaam   Hong Kong   Karachi
Kuala Lumpur   Madrid   Melbourne   Mexico City   Nairobi
New Delhi   Shanghai   Taipei   Toronto

With offices in
Argentina   Austria   Brazil   Chile   Czech Republic   France   Greece
Guatemala   Hungary   Italy   Japan   Poland   Portugal   Singapore
South Korea   Switzerland   Thailand   Turkey   Ukraine   Vietnam

Published by Oxford University Press, Inc.
198 Madison Avenue, New York, New York 10016

www.oup.com

Oxford is a registered trademark of Oxford University Press

Library of Congress Cataloging-in-Publication Data
Golden, Peter B.
Central Asia in world history / Peter B. Golden.
p. cm.
Summary: "This work traces the history of the nomadic steppe tribes and sedentary
inhabitants of the oasis city-states of Central Asia from pre-history to the present.
Particular focus is placed on the unique melting pot cultures that this region has
produced over millennia"— Provided by publisher.
ISBN 978-0-19-533819-5 (pbk.)—ISBN 978-0-19-515947-9 (hardcover : alk. paper)
1. Asia, Central—History. 2. Asia, Central—Civilization.
3. Asia, Central—Strategic aspects. 4. Geopolitics—Asia, Central—History.
I. Title.
DS329.4.G598 2011
958—dc22   2010020626

7   9   11   13   15   14   12   10   8   6

Printed in the United States of America

Frontispiece: A Kyrgyz grandmother with her grandchildren.
The Kyrgyz, like other Central Asian nomads, have a rich
history of rug making and embroidery.
ITAR-TASS

For Sylvia

Contents

Editors' Preface

This book is part of the New Oxford World History, an innovative series that offers readers an informed, lively, and up-to-date history of the world and its people that represents a significant change from the "old" world history. Only a few years ago, world history generally amounted to a history of the West—Europe and the United States—with small amounts of information from the rest of the world. Some versions of the "old" world history drew attention to every part of the world *except* Europe and the United States. Readers of that kind of world history could get the impression that somehow the rest of the world was made up of exotic people who had strange customs and spoke difficult languages. Still another kind of "old" world history presented the story of areas or peoples of the world by focusing primarily on the achievements of great civilizations. One learned of great buildings, influential world religions, and mighty rulers but little of ordinary people or more general economic and social patterns. Interactions among the world's peoples were often told from only one perspective.

This series tells world history differently. First, it is comprehensive, covering all countries and regions of the world and investigating the total human experience—even those of so-called peoples without histories living far from the great civilizations. "New" world historians thus share in common an interest in all of human history, even going back millions of years before there were written human records. A few "new" world histories even extend their focus to the entire universe, a "big history" perspective that dramatically shifts the beginning of the story back to the big bang. Some see the "new" global framework of world history today as viewing the world from the vantage point of the Moon, as one scholar put it. We agree. But we also want to take a close-up view, analyzing and reconstructing the significant experiences of all of humanity.

This is not to say that everything that has happened everywhere and in all time periods can be recovered or is worth knowing, but that there is much to be gained by considering both the separate and interrelated stories of different societies and cultures. Making these connections is still another crucial ingredient of the "new" world history. It emphasizes connectedness and interactions of all kinds—cultural, economic, political, religious, and social—involving peoples, places, and processes. It makes comparisons and finds similarities. Emphasizing both the comparisons and interactions is critical to developing a global framework that can deepen and broaden historical understanding, whether the focus is on a specific country or region or on the whole world.

The rise of the new world history as a discipline comes at an opportune time. The interest in world history in schools and among the general public is vast. We travel to one another's nations, converse and work with people around the world, and are changed by global events. War and peace affect populations worldwide as do economic conditions and the state of our environment, communications, and health and medicine. The New Oxford World History presents local histories in a global context and gives an overview of world events seen through the eyes of ordinary people. This combination of the local and the global further defines the new world history. Understanding the workings of global and local conditions in the past gives us tools for examining our own world and for envisioning the interconnected future that is in the making.

Bonnie G. Smith
Anand Yang

Central Asia in World History

A Layering of Peoples

Historically, Central Asians had no all-embracing term for the region or its peoples. The ties of clan, tribe, status, locale, or religion were the primary components of Central Asian identities, and these were often multi-layered. For its large nomadic population, political delimitations were of little consequence. Control over people brought control over territory.

For millennia a bridge between East and West, China, India, Iran, the Mediterranean lands, and more recently Russia have influenced Central Asia, the meeting ground of shamans, Buddhists, Zoroastrians, Jews, Christians, and Muslims, among others. Its shifting ethnic, linguistic, political and cultural borders encompassed two interacting yet fundamentally different lifeways, each inhabiting different ecological niches: the settled folk of its oases and the nomads of the steppes. Ancient and medieval observers considered it marginal to "civilization." Modern historians have deemed it the "heartland" or "pivot" of Eurasian history because it produced the largest empires of premodern times.

Central Asia occupies approximately one-seventh of Earth's landmass, some eight million square miles. Today, western Central Asia, overwhelmingly Muslim, consists of the newly independent states of the former Soviet Union: Turkmenistan, Uzbekistan, Kazakhstan, Kyrgyzstan, and Tajikistan, historically called "Western Turkestan[1]." Soviet policy determined the names and borders of the modern states, attempting, for the first time in history, to tie politically delineated territories to specific ethno-linguistic groups—often defining them according to political needs. Muslim Central Asia also includes Xinjiang (also called "Eastern Turkestan") in China, with its indigenous Uighur and other Turko-Muslim populations. Today, much of the region between the Amur Darya River and Xinjiang, once largely Iranian-speaking, is Turkic in language, a linguistic shift that has been in progress for 1500 years, creating a "Turko-Persian" cultural world. Southward,

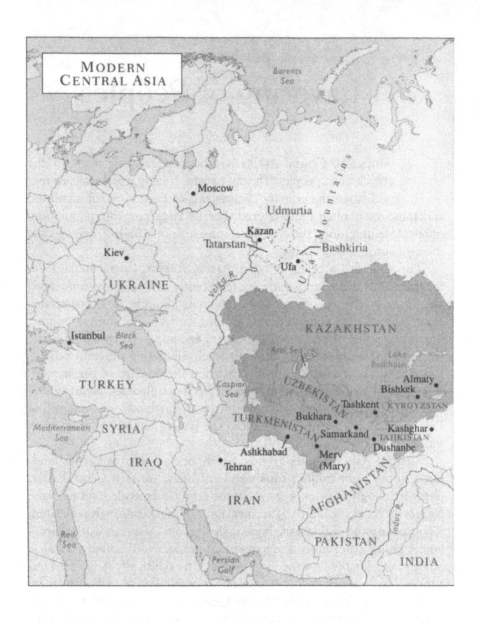

MODERN CENTRAL ASIA

Afghanistan, tied to its northern neighbors by ethnicity and language, is a microcosm of this mix.

Eastern Central Asia, largely Buddhist, comprises Mongolia, divided today into the Republic of Mongolia, the Inner Mongolian Autonomous Region of China, and Manchuria. Tibet, linguistically distinct from Central Asia, has, at various times, played a critical role in Central Asian affairs.

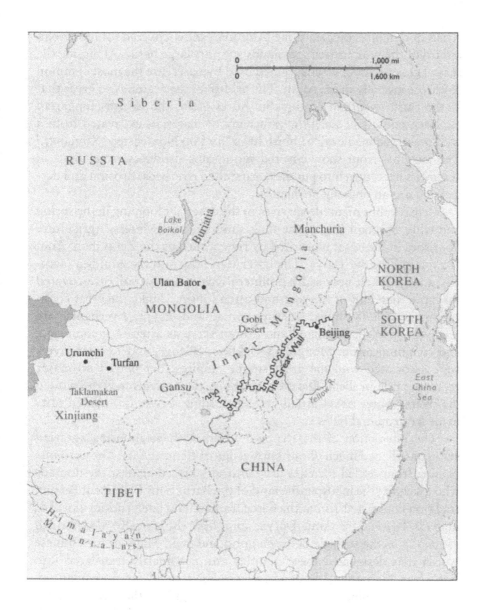

The forest-steppe zones between the Volga and western Siberia contain substantial Muslim Turkic populations with historical and cultural roots in Central Asia. Politically and culturally, Central Asia, an exporter of peoples, has also extended into Hungary, Ukraine, Russia, and the Middle East.

The steppe, a mix of prairie, desert and semi-desert extending from Hungary to the Altay Mountains and the Manchurian forests, is Central

Asia's dominant ecological zone. Although snow-covered for more than a third of the year, its rich grasslands support large herds. Alongside the seas of grass, baking deserts, punctuated by oases, are the most common feature, especially in the south. The aridity of the region is so great that in the early twentieth century Sir Aurel Stein, the British-Hungarian explorer, could still smell the pungency of materials excavated from a well-preserved medieval "rubbish heap" in Lop Nor (eastern Xinjiang).[2] The melt off from snow-covered mountains produces rivers that, in summer's heat, turn into puddles or parched riverbeds. Erosion and desiccation are an ongoing problem.

Remarkably, plant life survives in the deserts, blooming in the spring and lying dormant during the long summers and winters. Agriculture flourishes in the oases nourished by rivers, such as the Zeravshan, Amu Darya, and the Syr Darya. The latter two flow into the Aral Sea (actually a large lake), now sadly polluted. Rivers are partially ice-covered for more than half of the year and often longer. Unlike the great civilizations of China, India, Mesopotamia, and Egypt, riverbanks are relatively sparsely populated and do not serve as arteries of commerce and communication. Mongolia's Orkhon, Selenge, and Kerulen rivers were associated with the great steppe empires, but played no major economic role in them. Except for fishing, the nomads never exploited the rivers. Water travel usually meant fording a river on inflated rafts made from animal hides.

The interaction of the steppe-dwellers with neighboring agrarian states has shaped much of our knowledge of Central Asia. The accounts coming from settled societies are culturally biased against the nomads who dwelt in "the inhospitable land of the Barbarians."[3] Ancient Persian tradition contrasted *Turan*, the fierce Iranian (and later Turkic) world of nomads beyond the Amu Darya, and *Iran* (historically also termed "Persia"), as the struggle between good and evil.[4] Many of the Chinese words that designated these peoples are customarily translated into English as "barbarian," but these terms were actually far more nuanced, ranging in meaning from "vassal" and "foreign" to the less charitable "barbarous."[5] Chinese historians made no attempt to hide their revulsion at the nomads' "primitive" customs, cuisine, and clothing of animal hides, fur, and felt.

However, archaeological finds show that some nomads lived rich, even luxuriant lives, often confirmed by the same scornful contemporary observers. They lined their fur garments, necessary for the cold, with silk obtained from China and other precious textiles from Iran. They made extensive use of gold and gilded objects in their finery. The

Some 4,000 gold objects covering the remains of this high-ranking Saka, along with gold, silver, bronze, and wooden utensils, were found in a gravesite in southeastern Kazakhstan. Today, the "Golden Man" has become a national symbol of Kazakhstan. Courtesy of the Institute of Archaeology of the Ministry of Education and Science of the Republic of Kazakhstan

ceremonial costume of the "Golden Man" largely made from gold or decorated with golden articles, replete with a high golden headdress (such high headdresses were also common among women well into medieval times—indeed some archaeologists think that the so-called "Golden Man" may actually be a warrior priestess), shows that

"Barbarian" clothing, an early, all-gold version of a top hat and tails, was anything but primitive.[6] Nomads had a rich tradition of oral poetry, song and music. Some scholars credit them with the invention of bowed musical instruments, such as the violin, derived perhaps from the ancestor of the *qobïz* still played by Central Asian peoples such as the Kazakhs and Kyrgyz today. The oldest example of a "horse-head fiddle," called *morin khuur* in Mongol, dating to the seventh or eighth century was found in warrior's burial site in Mongolia in 2008.[7]

The themes of "barbarism" and the "noble savage" are common in the writings of ancient and medieval authors describing what they perceived as an alien world. In reality, the nomads were no more blood-thirsty or covetous of gold or silks than their "civilized" neighbors. Life on the steppe was harsh, but many nomads felt theirs was a superior existence to those who spent a lifetime in backbreaking labor on the soil. Urban Central Asia, with its rich and cosmopolitan culture and its agrarian and commerce-oriented economy, had a symbiotic relationship with its nomadic neighbors, often serving as the connecting bond between steppe and sown.

A key theme of Central Asian history is the movement of peoples and languages and the creation of new ethnic entities. Languages are usually grouped into "families" indicating origins in a common linguistic, but not necessarily biological, source. Two language families, Indo-European and Altaic, dominate the history of Central Asia. The Indo-Europeans formed a linguistic community that lived in the Black Sea steppes around 4500 to 4000 BCE. By 3000 or 2500 BCE, this community began to break up, with groups moving into central, south, and west Asia and the northern Mediterranean.[8] Their linguistic descendants extend from the Indic speakers of South Asia (Hindi-Urdu, Punjabi, and many other languages in the Indian subcontinent) and Iranian speakers of Iran, Afghanistan, and Central Asia (Persian, Tajik, Pashtun, and other Iranian languages) to the British Isles and include all of the languages of Europe except for Basque, Finnish, Estonian, and related Finnic languages, and Hungarian, its distant relative.

Altaic was located in Southern Siberia, eastern Mongolia, and Manchuria. Its members include Turkish and various Turkic tongues spoken in Central Asia, such as Uzbek, Kazakh, and Uighur, as well as Mongolian found in various forms in Mongolia, Inner Mongolia, and adjoining areas of China and Russia, including the Kalmyk people in the Volga region. Manchu (now nearly extinct) and the smaller Tungusic peoples of Manchuria constitute the eastern branch. Some scholars would include the ancestors of Korean and Japanese in the Altaic "family." Others not only reject this connection, but also contest the idea that Altaic constitutes a language family. Rather, they argue, the parallels between the different Altaic languages are merely the result of centuries of interaction and lexical borrowing.[9]

As the history of Central Asia amply demonstrates, medieval and modern "peoples" are often the product of many ethnic and linguistic layers mixed over time and brought together with no small measure of political calculation, especially in modern times. The means by which a language spread is not always clear. Conquest, mass migration, and the total displacement of one people by another is one model. Another is marked by gradual infiltration, interaction, and resultant bilingualism. Migrating groups are themselves often the products of extensive ethnic and linguistic interaction. With each new movement, the ethnic name and the changing language associated with that name will be passed on to another grouping, in a relay-race fashion. The result is that peoples bearing the same name and speaking forms of a common language may actually have

The two strings of the Kazakh and Kyrgyz qobïz are made of horsehair. Shamans played this instrument as part of their healing ceremonies. Commission mongole pour l'UNESCO © UNESCO

multiple and diverse origins. The movement of peoples has produced an intricate mosaic. The ethno-linguistic map that we see today is merely a snapshot, at a given point in time, of blendings that have been taking place over millennia. The creation of peoples is an ongoing process.

The Rise of Nomadism and Oasis City-States

Modern human beings (*Homo sapiens*), whose origins lie in Africa, entered Central Asia about 40,000 years ago during the Ice Age, probably in pursuit of game. By about 10,000–8000 BCE, with climate conditions resembling those of today, perhaps 500,000 humans out of a global population of about 10 million inhabited Central Asia-Siberia. There were several migration routes, one via the Middle East, another going to East Asia, and others from there to Central Asia. Agriculture developed by 6000 BCE. It may have originated both locally and through the movement of agriculturalists from other areas, in particular the Middle East and Europe, who came to the southwestern fringe of Central Asia (modern Turkmenistan). They grew wheat and barley. Development was discontinuous; settlements were abandoned.

Some 3,000 years later, the building of irrigation canals secured a more reliable basis for agriculture and further population growth. Contacts developed with Elam (southwestern Iran) and Sumerian Mesopotamia to the west, and with Afghanistan and India to the east. Some settlements appear to have had connections with or perhaps even derived from the Harappan civilization (about 3000–2000 BCE) of the Indus valley (northwestern India and Pakistan). Early Dravidian peoples, now concentrated in southern India, may have spread across the southern rim of Central Asia, producing a series of settlements from India to Iran, including perhaps even Elam, although this remains debated. Today, the nearly one million Brahui found in eastern Iran, southern Afghanistan, and Pakistan may be the remnants of a pre-historic Dravidian layer of peoples in the Central Asian ethnic mosaic. There were, undoubtedly, other still-unidentified peoples that settled in this vast expanse as well. For example, linguistic evidence suggests that the Burushaski language in northern Pakistan, unrelated to any of the languages surrounding it, may have affiliations with languages spoken in Daghestan in the northeastern Caucasus, although this hypothesis is not universally accepted. The ethnic pre-history of Central Asia and its early linkages with and between the Indian subcontinent and the Middle East have yet to be fully elucidated. Goods passed between the scattered settlements, producing trading contacts between India, Iran, and Mesopotamia through Central Asia. In the course of the late third millennium BCE, towns arose in Turkmenistan with populations engaged in irrigated farming, handicrafts, and metallurgy. They developed organized religious institutions attested by the ziggurat temple dedicated to the Moon God at Altïn-Depe, about a three-hour drive southeast of Ashkhabad (Ashghabat), the capital of Turkmenistan. Evidence for early writing systems influenced by Elam, Sumeria, and Harappa has also been found on seals, which were used to mark objects used by rulers and priests. This early urban culture, with its writing and indications of social divisions, declined between the late second- and early first-millennium BCE, perhaps due to over-farming or disastrous climate changes. In the first millennium BCE, Iranian peoples migrated here, most probably from the Black Sea steppes or from more northern parts of Central Asia.

Hunter-gatherer and fishing populations inhabited much of the area north of the agricultural communities in southern Turkmenistan in the sixth to fourth millennia BCE. The steppes with their vast grassy plains became more inviting to those early agriculturalists, who placed greater emphasis on livestock breeding. The process cannot be traced with certainty because of the scarcity of data. People changed the emphasis of their economic pursuits as they moved into new lands. The domestication of the horse, perhaps as early as 4800 BCE (the dating is hotly debated), most probably in the Ponto-Caspian steppes, was certainly a turning point. Horses were first a source of food. By about 4000 BCE, herdsmen-consumers had become more adept at exploiting their animals for a wider range of purposes beyond food. They used their hides for clothing and dwellings and harnessed their strength as "beasts of burden." They began to ride them, perhaps before 3700 BCE,[1] and sacrificed them to their deities. By 2000 BCE some subsistence agriculturalists, having become largely if not wholly dependent on their herds, engaged in seasonal migrations to established pastures in the steppe. They became pastoral nomads. Many retained elements of other technologies, such as agriculture, irrigation, and metallurgy, the latter quite advanced in the Urals and elsewhere. They alternated along an adaptive scale of low to high technology as circumstances required—as do present day pastoral nomads.

Some scholars suggest that the transition to pastoral nomadism originated in the western steppes. Others argue that it took place independently in both the western and eastern steppes or among reindeer herders in the South Siberian and Manchurian forests who adapted their skills to live-stock management in the steppe. Our picture of the process is constantly changing with new archaeological discoveries and new, often contradic-tory, interpretations of the evidence. No one is sure exactly where or pre-cisely why full pastoral nomadism first evolved. Climate change, a growing demand for livestock, security concerns, and new technologies may have all played a role. In the third millennium BCE, the number of livestock-breeders and their herds began to grow. They moved further into the steppe, and herding became their primary occupation. Hunting, of course, continued to be an important source of food. This remained true of the later nomads as well. Organized hunts also served as a form of military training. By the early second millennium (about 1700–1500 BCE), a horse-back-riding population had clearly emerged among some of the steppe-dwelling stock-herders. Horses and oxen hauled the carts and wagons on which their portable dwellings were perched, much like the covered wagons of the American West, as they migrated from pasturage to pas-turage with their herds. The composition of the herds also changed, greater preference being given to horses and sheep, which were better adapted to longer migrations. Horses came to make up as much as 36% of the total livestock. The harnessing of horsepower had other, more ominous, mili-tary consequences, contributing to a turbulent period of migrations in the steppes of the Indo-Europeans, who brought equestrian-based warfare with them. The process unfolded in two stages. First, wheeled carts and then war-chariots, perhaps invented in Central Asia, appeared. Early types dating to about 2000 BCE were found at Sintashta, a heavily fortified settlement in the southern Urals steppe zone, part of the Sintashta-Arkaim-Petrovka archaeological complex. Sintashta, with its well-developed metallurgy (indicating, perhaps, armament production and a more milita-rized age) was part of a growing network of urban settlements in this part of the steppe. Soviet scholars dubbed it "the Country of Towns." By the second millennium BCE, war-chariots made their way into China and the Middle East.

The second stage is connected with the invention of the compound or composite bow, composed of wood, animal horn, and sinews. It rev-olutionized warfare on the steppe because it was powerful, relatively small and—most importantly—could be fired with ease in all directions while on horseback. Its origins may go back to Egypt in the early third millennium BCE, but others date it to about 1000 BCE. By that time in the Eurasian steppes, sporadic mounted raiders had become disciplined cavalry, organized into armies with ideologies extolling the warrior as part of a trained group, rather than glory-seeking individual combatants (although those were not lacking). The chariot became yesterday's technology.[2] The accompanying spread of iron weapons heightened warfare as mounted horsemen more systematically raided their neighbors in the steppe and sought access to the products of the settled world. Warfare, now requiring more extensive forms of organization, led to the rise of large tribal unions.

The nomads, masters of horse-borne mobility (and possessing a large amount of the world's horsepower), became fearsome warriors whose lightning-like raids and clouds of arrows terrified their victims. Their modes of warfare changed little over millennia. They went to war with five or more horses, frequently switching mounts in the course of a battle. This often deceived their opponents as to their true numbers and gave them the ability to launch continuous fresh attacks. When faced with stronger or equally capable opponents, nomads saw no dishonor in quickly leaving a battle. Even then, they were still a threat as they could fire their arrows with deadly accuracy facing backwards. Moreover, feigned retreats that led into ambushes were a favorite stratagem.

This warrior society depended on highly organized strategies of stockbreeding, some entailing lengthy seasonal migrations (full nomadism). Others were semi-nomads, primarily agriculturalists, but engaging in minimal migrations. Migrations were not aimless wanderings in search of water and grass, as outsiders reported, but followed carefully planned and defended routes and pastures. Herd size and the mix of sheep, horses, cattle, camels, goats, and yaks varied according to local ecologies. These factors also determined the number of dependent humans. Unlike agrarian societies, nomadism is not labor-intensive and does not require large populations for production purposes. One or two shepherds on foot can handle flocks of hundreds of sheep. A single rider can manage considerably larger flocks or even a herd of 100 or more horses.

Nomadic livestock breeding was a family business. As their herds needed extensive pasturage, nomads camped in small units, usually four to five families, often related. When additional hands were needed, a family called on kinsmen. Slavery, known in nomadic society since antiquity, was usually limited to a few domestic slaves, mainly individuals captured during raids. Today, a herd of about 100 animals can sustain the average nomad household, typically consisting of five people (father, mother, two children and one grandparent). The same was probably true of the past. Ancient and medieval accounts provide little information on the nomads' family life. Modern ethnographers describe a highly ordered, patriarchal society with rigid social rules within the household. For

Many Kyrgyz nomads engage in vertical rather than horizontal migrations, moving from valleys where they winter to mountain ranges, where there are fresh grass and water, in the summer. Ergun Çağatay / Tetragon A. S.

example, modern Turkmen newlyweds cannot speak or eat in front of their in-laws and other older relatives. Young wives, acquired through the payment of a bride-price (or kidnapped), gained a better standing within the family after giving birth to several sons, as males are considered the bearers of the lineage. Daughters are merely "guests" who will in time go off to other families. The Turkmen take great pride in their ancestry and can recite the names of their forebears for many generations.[3]

The wealthy occasionally supported poorer kinsmen in distress. If their fortunes did not change, the latter either became more dependent or gave up nomadism and settled down as farmers. This was considered a great loss of status. Desperate nomads such as these provided willing recruits for the war-bands of local chieftains. Wealth was measured in horses and sheep, the latter constituting the largest number of livestock. Sheep are hardy and easily managed, and they provide meat, hides, and wool. Horses were the most prized and prestigious components of the herd, providing meat, milk, and transport. They were critical to the nomad's management of his economy and his dealings with the outside world. They provided mobility, the nomad's principal advantage in combat. Camels (the two-humped Bactrian variety), especially useful for transport in the desert and semi-desert zone, were relatively common.

Goats, not highly esteemed, were usually associated with poorer nomads. Cattle were kept in more limited numbers. Animal diseases, the vagaries of climate, and especially the dreaded *jut* (frosts that followed a thaw), could deplete herds. Although 60 to 90 percent of the fertile females might bear young in a year, mortality rates were high, ranging from 30 to 60 percent. Nomads, when they had a surplus, traded it with townspeople for foodstuffs, clothing, and weapons, some accumulating considerable wealth.

The nomads moved their herds from one pasturage to another, in the different seasonal quarters. Winter in the steppe is the most difficult season. Areas that could provide shelter from the elements, such as valleys, mountainsides away from the winds, or areas near forests were favored for the winter camps. Because of this, some forests were considered holy lands and refuges. Nomads also clustered around riverbanks, fishing during the non-migrating period. The summer camps were preferably in the uplands, near sources of fresh water that often dry up in the baking plains. Migrations were generally southward in winter and northward in summer. The length of the distances traveled varied. Those engaged in "horizontal" migrations moved across the steppe, often traveling hundreds of miles. Others, practicing a kind of "vertical" nomadism, drove their herds up and down mountains, traversing considerably shorter distances. Migratory routes were possessions of a clan or tribe. Struggles for pasturage could produce a kind of domino effect pushing some tribes into the sedentary world. It was in such instances that the historical sources usually record them.

Outside observers continually underscored the nomad's greed and covetousness (while ignoring their own). In reality, nomadic interactions with the sedentary world were not based on avarice nor were they unremittingly hostile. Relations could even be symbiotic. Owen Lattimore, an American scholar, traveler, old "China hand," and one-time caravanner in North China and Mongolia wrote, "it is the poor nomad who is the pure nomad."[4] Although it is possible for nomads to sustain themselves on their meat and dairy products and some limited agriculture (indeed, ancient nomads may have been better fed than ancient farmers[5]), they also wanted access to the clothing; liquor and comestibles; and artifacts of gold, silver, and precious stones produced by settled societies. Moreover, the latter were an important source of other manufactured goods, especially weapons (although nomad metalworkers were quite capable here too) and inventions that directly benefited the nomadic way of life.

For example, breast straps for horses and the compound bow came from the sedentary world. Iron stirrups, so closely associated with the equestrian way of life, may have entered Central Asia from East Asia (earlier stirrups were made of less durable organic materials such as animal hides). The dating of their precise point of origin and transmission is contested. Taking this into account, it can be argued that the "pure" nomad, at least in historical times, lacking access to the sedentary world, was often the poorer nomad. Access was usually based on power relationships. For nomads, raiding or trading were alternate strategies to the same end. They chose whichever was most cost-efficient. Their neighbors, especially China, attempted to control nomad behavior by opening or closing frontier markets.

Nomad relations with the settled world required someone who could speak for the group (clan, tribe, or people). This meant political organization. In a society lacking permanent borders, kinship, real and "invented," provided the most important political bond. The nomads were organized in "clans" and "tribes" (unions of clans), terms that outsiders often understood imprecisely. Theoretically, all members of a clan descended from a common ancestor. All clans in a tribe descended from a more distant common ancestor. In reality, these ties were much more fluid, being created and forgotten as political necessity dictated. Tribes often formed confederations, usually adopting the name of the politically dominant tribe. When these unions disintegrated, they often reformed in a slightly altered configuration under the name of the new dominant tribe.

Statehood was not the normal condition in steppe society. Nomad political organization, responding to military aggression or internal crises provoked by the attempts of neighboring states to manipulate their internal affairs, oscillated between empire and various forms of stateless confederation. The lure of China's wealth and the occasional projection of its power into the steppes could push the nomads towards state formation. Such stimuli were largely lacking in the western steppes. Nomadic states here invariably came from the eastern steppes. Nomads did not normally seek to conquer settled societies. Similarly, neighboring empires, such as China and pre-Islamic Iran, only infrequently ventured into the steppe. Such campaigns were costly and hazardous. China and Byzantium preferred bribery, diplomacy, and the use of "barbarians to attack barbarians."[6]

When nomads did conquer sedentary lands, they produced powerful ruling houses that quickly took on the trappings of settled dynastic empires, and they sought to transform their nomadic followers into settled subjects. This was not the reward that rank-and-file nomads sought. Conquest by the nomads, in turn, often reshaped some political institutions of the settled peoples, with the nomads superimposing elements of their political culture on the already existing institutions of the conquered state.

Nomad empires began by first conquering other nomads, incorporating them into often uneasy tribal unions. Ethnically diverse and polyglot, nomadic states were filled with competing forces. There were aristocrats and commoners. Certain clans ranked higher than others. A clan or tribal chief was expected to share some of his wealth with his followers. Stingy leaders lost followers—and sometimes their lives. Unwilling subject peoples rebelled.

Commerce also brought people together over large distances. Inclusion into the expanding Achaemenid Persian Empire (559–330 BCE) drew Central Asia into the transcontinental trade of the Ancient World. In the early Middle Ages, it became the central link in the Silk Road, a network of often-shifting caravan routes connecting the cities of Eurasia. It brought the goods of China, in particular silk, westward through Central Asia to Iran. Iran sold the goods at very considerable profit throughout the Mediterranean world. China, the technological powerhouse of the pre-modern world, in turn imported an array of exotic goods and foodstuffs from Central Asia (such as the much-prized "golden peaches of Samarkand") and from lands to the west (such as lions from Iran).[7]

The nomads of the Great Steppe protected these crucial avenues of commerce. The routes were dangerous, especially through the deserts, which were littered with the bleached skeletons of men and beasts. Mongolia has the Gobi (which in Mongol means desert), Xinjiang the much-feared Taklamakan (second in size only to the Sahara), and Turkmenistan the Qara Qum (Black Sands). Even today, Turkmen parents sew little bells on the clothes of their children so that they can be located in the shifting sands.[8] Occasionally, the winds shift the sand dunes to reveal the vestiges of ancient buildings.[9] The Taklamakan is hard to reach and even harder to exit. According to a folk etymology, Taklamakan means "once you enter, you cannot leave." In Turfan (pronounced Turpan by its Modern Uighur inhabitants), summer temperatures can soar as high as 78°C / 128°F. Quintus Curtius, a first- to early second-century CE Roman historian of the campaigns of Alexander the Great in the Sogdian deserts (in Uzbekistan), reported that the summer's heat made the sands glow, and "everything is burned as if by continuous conflagration," leaving the conqueror's troops

Darius the Great, who expanded Achaemenid Persian power to Central Asia, is depicted hunting lions by chariot. Hunting was more than a sport for rulers. It was a demonstration of their power over the natural world. Werner Forman / Art Resource, New York

"parched."[10] Nonetheless, merchants and pilgrims with their religions, alphabets, technologies, and numerous other artifacts of culture, entertainment, goods and gadgets, traversed the east-west steppe highways.

The nomads actively promoted long-distance commerce, as both middlemen and bearers of elements of their own culture to the wider world. Certain types of clothing (perhaps trousers), stringed instruments, and equine paraphernalia probably came from the steppe. As a result of early contacts, steppe peoples figure in the ethnographic legends of the ancient world contributing to the European cultural heritage. For example, the participation of steppe women in warfare may have played a role in shaping the Greek legends of the Amazons. Women in the steppe world wielded political power.

Early nomads shunned Central Asian cities except as sources of desired goods. Yet, paradoxically, it was the nomadic factor that brought these oasis city-states into larger political units. Otherwise, given the constraints of distance and security, their most common form of political organization was a loose union. The Transoxanian oases were essentially Iranian-speaking, independent-minded, cosmopolitan, aristocratic, mercantile city-states, each ruled by a lord who was simply the "first among equals." Business-oriented and rich, the city-states produced vibrant cultures that reflected their transcontinental business and intellectual interests. They did not aspire to political domination, but to commercial and cultural exchange. Their merchants, bureaucrats, and men of religion, however, became major contributors to the administrative and cultural life of the steppe empires. According to a medieval Turkic saying, "a Turk is never without a Persian [*Tat*, a sedentary Iranian], just as a cap is never without a head."[11] The relationship was mutually beneficial.

The Turko-Mongolian nomads gave rise to few durable cities. In Central Asia, the great cities were largely the work of Iranian peoples. Of the Old Turkic words for "city," one, *kend/kent*, is clearly a borrowing from Iranian (*kand* or *qand*, as in Samarkand). Another, *balïq*, is of disputed origin.[12] Mongol *balghasun* (town, city) stems from the same term and was probably borrowed from ancient Turkic. Cities built by nomads were largely outgrowths of the *ordu* (also *orda*, *ordo*), a word in use since Xiongnu times, which initially meant "the camp of the ruler." Its meaning was expanded to denote the capital city, and, as the ruler was invariably accompanied by his military forces, *ordu* came to mean "army" as well (English "horde" derives from it). Such "cities" usually had few structures made of durable materials such as clay or brick, but were rather conglomerations of people, including resident foreign merchants, living in the tents of the nomads. As a consequence, these "cities" are difficult to trace archaeologically.

Nomad rulers also took control over genuine cities that stemmed from fortified oasis settlements created by earlier Iranian tribes, some of which had taken up settled life by about 500 BCE. Muslim geographers and historians from the ninth to tenth centuries describe these towns, including their stout walls, gates, the distances between them, and the roads leading to them. They also highlight mosques and other religious or cultural structures and local products, all matters of considerable interest to the readers of that day. Archaeologists have been carrying out investigations of cities such as Bukhara, Samarkand, and Tashkent (earlier called Chach) for many years. Travelers' accounts also give some information about their size. By modern standards, they were not very large. According to Xuanzang, the seventh-century Chinese traveler and Buddhist pilgrim, Samarkand was about twenty *li* in size, or about seven kilometers. Its town center was about two square kilometers.

Many of these cities followed similar patterns. They were divided into sections, best known by medieval Persian or Arabic terminology.

The military-political core was the *ark/arq*, also called *kuhandîz/quhandîz* (sometimes shortened to *kundûz* or *kundîz*), a Persian word meaning "old fort" or "citadel," often rendered in Arabic by *qal'a* (fort, stronghold), usually located within the town center. Here, the rulers lived in a castle along with their personal guard and military commanders. The treasury, chancellery, a temple for the local (pre-Islamic era) cult, and even a prison were within its confines. By the time the Muslim geographers began to write about the cities, many of these citadels lay in ruins—hence the term "old fort" used for them. Energetic, later rulers often rebuilt them—a form of urban renewal for the elite. Many smaller urban settlements also had a *kuhandîz*.

The town center was termed *shahristân*, another Persian word deriving from *shahr* (city; in Arabic *madîna*). In Bukhara and Penjikent, however, the *kuhandîz* lay outside the walls of the *shahristân*, forming its own political-military-administrative center. The outlying suburbs were called *rabaḍ* an Arabic word which is different than the similar sounding Arabic *rabaṭ* (plural *ribâṭ*) initially a term for forts, bristling with "fighters for the faith," that guarded the frontiers and raided the pagan Turkic nomads. *Ribâṭ* also came to mean "caravansary," the medieval equivalent of a motel for travelers and merchants. *Rabaḍ* could also denote the wall that girded the town center and suburbs.

Agricultural settlements, termed *rustak/rustâq*, surrounded the cities. They produced the melons for which Central Asia was famous, as well as fruits, grapes, vegetables, grains, and other food products. Cloth production, ceramics, glassware, and the manufacture of a host of utensils, ranging from cookware to weapons, were also an important part of the economy. Archaeological excavations of cities such as Taraz (in Kazakhstan) and Samarkand show that the designs on the products often catered to the stylistic preferences of the neighboring nomads as well as the local urban population. For example, seals on gemstones from ancient Samarkand (the archaeological site Afrasiyab) have two different styles: one depicting a bull with wings, reflecting the mythological subject matter preferred by the townsmen, the other a goat in flight with an arrow in his neck, an example of the scenes of the hunt so dear to the nomads. Cities near rich ore deposits in nearby mountains became both mining and production centers for bronze, iron, gold, and silver manufactures.

The cities were not merely stopping points on the Silk Road, but also major contributors to the goods that flowed across the steppes. Some merchants became extremely wealthy and had grand homes, the equal of the local rulers, that ostentatiously displayed their wealth.

Samarkand was one of the key cities of pre-Islamic and Islamic Central Asia, with roots going back to at least 500 BCE. When Alexander the Great in 329 BCE conquered "Marakanda," as the Greeks called it, it was already a thriving city. Narshakhî, writing in the 940s his *History of Bukhara*, another great city of the region, claimed that its citadel was founded 3,000 years earlier.

Urban and agrarian Central Asia distinguished between different social orders, aristocrats and commoners. When Turkic-speaking nomads replaced the earlier Iranian nomads, from the third to fourth century onwards, a linguistic divide was added. Nonetheless, the cities adapted. They needed the nomads to facilitate their trade and to protect them from other nomads. It is this interaction on all levels of political, economic, social and cultural life that constitutes a continuing theme of Central Asian history.

CHAPTER TWO

The Early Nomads:
"Warfare Is Their Business"

The breakup of the Indo-European linguistic community around 3000 to 2500 BCE produced an outpouring of peoples across Eurasia and adjoining lands. One grouping, the ancestors of the Tokharians, arrived in Xinjiang by the late third- or early second-millennium BCE,[1] making it one of the most ancient and enduring points of Chinese contact with Western peoples. Another grouping, the Indo-Iranians or Indo-Aryans, also went eastward to Siberia, Mongolia, Xinjiang, and northern Pakistan. The tribal name *Ârya/Âriya* (Aryan) derives from an Indo-European term meaning "lord, free person" and, ultimately, "a master of a house who shows hospitality to a stranger."[2] It did not have any of the racial connotations it acquired in the 20th century. By 2000 BCE, at the latest, the Indo-Iranians, who were agriculturalists and livestock breeders, had split into the linguistic ancestors of the Indic-speaking populations of South Asia and the Iranian-speaking populations of Iran and Central Asia today.

Indo-Aryans, probably coming through Afghanistan, entered South Asia around 1500 BCE, encountering the older Harappan civilization and Dravidian peoples. It was earlier thought that this was a sudden, mass invasion that dislocated, destroyed, or enslaved the earlier inhabitants. More recent scholarship suggests that this interaction was more gradual and peaceful, as the newcomers took over regions that had long been in decline.[3] Iranian-speaking tribes entered the land that now bears their name sometime between 1500 BCE and 1000 BCE, imposing themselves on a diverse population. In Ancient Persian, they may have called their new homeland *âryânâm khshathram* (the kingdom of the Aryans). In early medieval Persian this became *Êrânshahr* and later simply *Irân*.[4]

Other Indo-Iranians en route to Siberia made contacts with the Uralic northern forest peoples (linguistic ancestors of the Finns and Hungarians, among others) leaving traces of their interaction in words such as Hungarian *tehen* (cow) from Indo-Iranian *dhainu*, Finnish *parsas* (pig) from Indo-Iranian *parsa*, Finnish *mete* and Hungarian *méz* (honey) from Indo-Iranian *madhu*.[5] Subsequently, Iranian nomads made contact with

Turkic and other Altaic peoples in Mongolia and Siberia. Whether they introduced nomadism to them remains unclear. It is with the movements of these peoples that we move from pre-history to history, relying now not only on the surviving fragments of daily life unearthed by archaeologists, but also on the recorded observations of their neighbors.

In Central Asia, the Iranian nomads, whom the Persians called *Saka* and the Greeks *Scythians*, became an essential link between the growing civilizations of the Middle East and China. Nonetheless, crucial tools such as writing, central to the development of settled societies, do not appear to have come to the steppe until well into the first millennium CE. The agricultural revolution that spurred population growth elsewhere found only spotty reflection here. The nomads were best known for their martial prowess exhibited in their archery from horseback or a war chariot. In Old Iranian, the term *rathaeshtar* (aristocrat/warrior) literally meant "he who stands in a chariot."

The ancient Iranians believed that all things, even abstract ideas, possessed a living spirit. They made offerings to gods of water, fire, and other elements. Believers also imbibed an intoxicant, *haoma* (Sanskrit: *soma*) made from ephedra. Warriors seeking to achieve a state of ecstatic frenzy for combat partook of this stimulant. A special class of priests performed purification rites daily. The maintenance of ritual purity was essential to preserving *asha*, the natural order of the world and cosmos. *Asha* governed sunrise, sunset, the seasons, and justice. Humans were created to contribute to this by struggling for truth and justice and against the Lie (*drug*) and Evil.

Zoroaster (*Zarathushtra* in Old Iranian, which means "cameldriver"), the religious reformer after whom the Zoroastrian religion is named, most probably lived in Central Asia in the upper Amu Darya region, perhaps about 1200–1000 BCE (some scholars date him as early as 1500 BCE or as late 600 BCE; others place him in northwest Iran). In this "expanse of the Aryans" (*âryânâm vaêjô*), Zoroaster emphasized the ethical base of ancient Iranian beliefs, exalting Ahura Mazda (Lord Wisdom) as the Supreme Being and ruler of the forces of the Good. He heads the struggle against Ahriman, the leader of the demonic forces, a figure akin to the Judeo-Christian-Islamic concept of the Devil. Zoroaster underscored human responsibility to fight Evil. He believed that he received his prophetic revelations at the beginning of the last of four 3000-year cycles. After him, a savior-like figure will appear every 1000 years. The last of them, born of Zoroaster's miraculously preserved seed, will usher in the final struggle with Ahriman, the Day of Judgment, the end of days, and the attainment of paradise for the good. These

The Scythians, expert equestrians, employed their horses in war and in sport. Hare hunting, conducted on horseback at breakneck speed with short lances, was particularly popular and is often depicted in Scythian art. Erich Lessing / Art Resource, New York

ideas did not immediately win over his compatriots, but would have a profound impact on Judaism, Christianity, and Islam.

Subsequently, the Sasanid rulers of Persia made Zoroastrianism the official religion of their empire, but it never acquired this status in a Central Asian state. In Iran, there was also a hereditary priestly class closely associated with the monarchy, the *magu* in Old Persian, descended from the priest-tribe of the Medes, a kindred Iranian-speaking people, who dominated Iran and adjoining areas from 728 BCE until the Persians under Cyrus, the founder of the Persian Achaemenid Empire, conquered them in 550 BCE. Zoroastrianism is sometimes called the "Religion of the Magi." In Central Asia, Zoroastrianism, also termed Mazdaism or Mazdayasnaism (Mazda worship), incorporated elements from local beliefs and other religious traditions.

These ideas do not appear to have affected the Iranian Scythians (late eighth- to fourth-century BCE), the Sarmatians who supplanted them, or later Iranian nomadic tribes, which formed a series of confederations stretching from Ukraine to Mongolia. Herodotus considered the Scythians militarily invincible. According to him, they drank the blood of their slain foes, whose heads they brought to their king. The warriors fashioned napkins and clothing from the scalps of those they had killed and made drinking goblets from their skulls. Scythians swore oaths by consuming a mixture of blood (contributed by the oath-takers) and wine into which they first dipped their arrows or other weapons. In annual tribal or clan gatherings, those who had killed their enemies were permitted to join the chief in drinking a specially brewed wine. Those that had not were barred from participation in this ceremony, a signal dishonor.

Herodotus reports that the kindred Issedones consumed the flesh of their deceased fathers, mixing it with chopped sheep and goat meat. The deceased's head was then cleaned and gilded, serving afterwards "as a sacred image" to which they made sacrifices annually. Alien customs aside, Herodotus notes that they "observe rules of justice strictly" and women enjoy "equal power" with men.[6] Strabo, a Greek geographer in the first century BCE, says much the same of the kindred "uncouth, wild, and warlike" Massagetae, who are "in their business dealings, straightforward and not given to deceit."[7] The "animal style" art of the later Scythians, with its realistic and dramatic depictions of animals, expressed their love of the hunt and the natural world. The Scythians believed that animals possessed magical powers and they decorated their clothing, everyday objects, and weapons with animal images.

Meanwhile, other Iranians settled in some of the oases and fertile river valleys, forming the Sogdian and Khwarazmian peoples in what is today Uzbekistan and the Bactrians in Afghanistan. Yet others, such as the Khotanese Saka, went further east and established themselves in a number of oasis city-states in Xinjiang. Although dispersed across Central Asia, the various Iranian peoples retained much in common. Sima Qian, the "grand historian" of China, reports that the Iranians from Ferghana (eastern Uzbekistan and adjoining parts of Tajikistan and Kyrgyzstan) to Iran share "generally similar" customs and speak "mutually intelligible" languages. "They are skillful at commerce and will haggle over a fraction of a cent. Women are held in great respect, and the men make decisions on the advice of their women."[8] Overall, information about them is sparse. There may have been some loose political structures centering on Khwarazm (western Uzbekistan) and

Bactria (Afghanistan). Living on the borders of the steppe world and familiar with the nomads, Bactrians, Khwarazmians, and especially Sogdians were in an excellent position to serve as middlemen in trade.

Cyrus, the Persian who founded the first great land empire, extending from the Near East to northern India, invaded Central Asia. He subjugated Bactria, Sogdia, and Khwarazm, but subsequently perished in 530 BCE while leading a campaign against the Scythians. The Scythian queen, Tomyris, seeking revenge for her son's death, placed Cyrus's head in "a skin with human blood"[9] and declared that now the blood-thirsty conqueror could quench his thirst. Darius I, who came to power eight years after Cyrus's ghastly demise, was unable to conquer Greece but succeeded in Central Asia, subjugating some of the steppefolk. Margiana (modern Turkmenistan), Sogdia, Khwarazm, and Bactria, reached accommodations with the Achaemenids becoming *satrapies* (provinces) of the Persian Empire until Alexander the Great conquered the region in 330–329 BCE. The Scythians and later Iranian nomads, however, remained independent. Under Achaemenid rule, Iranian Central Asia became involved in long-distance trade networks connecting western and southern Asia. Trade furthered urban development and the expansion of agriculture, irrigated by large-scale canal systems. A system of underground irrigation canals called *kârîz* (a Persian term), even today an important feature of agriculture in Xinjiang, may have begun during the era of Achaemenid influence in Central Asia.[10] Ancient Persia pioneered this kind of canal, today called in Iran by its Arabic name, *qanât*.

Alexander's conquest of Iran (331–330 BCE) and his campaigns in Central Asia brought Khwarazm, Sogdia, and Bactria under Graeco-Macedonian rule. As elsewhere, Alexander founded or renamed a number of cities in his honor, such as Alexandria Eschate ("Outermost Alexandria," near modern Khojent in Tajikistan). He married Roxane, the daughter of a local Bactrian chieftain,[11] in the hope of creating closer bonds with the Iranian East. Alexander IV, his son with Roxane, never achieved full power. The squabbling Graeco-Macedonian generals killed them both in 309 and then divided the empire. By the mid-third century BCE, the Graeco-Macedonian colonists in Bactria broke away, creating their own state in the more northerly parts of Afghanistan.

The cultural history of Graeco-Bactria, with its rich blend of Hellenistic, Iranian, and Indian artistic traditions is partially known through fragmentary archaeological finds. Buddhism brought by missionaries from India had some success here. Politically, Graeco-Bactria expanded into northern India, Ferghana, and perhaps parts of Xinjiang.

Hand-dug canals in Xinjiang require constant attention. Typically, villagers dig a series of narrow but deep wells, sometimes to depths of 275 feet or more. The wells are linked by channels forming a kind of grand canal from which they build branches across the areas to be irrigated. Courtesy of Justin J. Rudelson

Weakened by Saka raiders and domestic strife, it declined by the mid-second century BCE. In 128 BCE, if not earlier, nomadic tribes coming from the Iranian and Tokharian borderlands of northern China overran it. The cause of these movements across the steppe was the rise and expansion of a new power in Mongolia: the Xiongnu.

The Xiongnu, whose origins are obscure, emerged in the third century BCE as China was recovering from a long period of internal strife that ended when the Qin (221–206 BCE) unified the various Chinese states. The Qin and their successors, the Han dynasty (202 BCE–220 CE) pursued an aggressive northern policy. They built fortification walls that would later become the Great Wall, a means to secure newly subjugated territories and a platform for further expansion. The Xiongnu saw this as a threat and prepared for war.[12] Sima Qian claimed that "plundering and marauding" was their response to crises. "Warfare," he concluded, "is their business."[13] They organized their army in units of 10, 100, 1000, and 10,000, divided into right and left wings with the commander at the

Eucratides I the Great, who issued numerous coins, was, according to Strabo, master of a thousand cities—probably an exaggeration. He appears to have seized power, touching off a civil war among the ever-fractious power holders in the Graeco-Bactrian kingdom and contributing, not long after his death, to its demise.
www.ancientsculpturegallery.com

center. This form of decimal military organization was widespread across the Central Asian nomadic world.

Qin incursions into Xiongnu pasturelands in the Ordos (in Inner Mongolia) in 215 BCE had driven their ruler, the *Chanyu* (supreme leader or emperor) Touman northward, unsettling the steppe. A subordinate of the Yuezhi, another nomadic people (most probably of Scythian or Tokharian origin) controlling Gansu and parts of Xinjiang and Mongolia, Touman had sent his oldest son Modun as a hostage to the Yuezhi court, a guarantee of Xiongnu good behavior. Modun correctly feared treachery from his father, who favored his younger half-brother as his successor. Touman suddenly attacked, perhaps hoping that the enraged Yuezhi would kill Modun in retaliation. Modun managed a daring escape and, as a reward for his courage, his father gave him a troop of 10,000 cavalry. Modun trained this troop to absolute obedience, ordering them to "shoot wherever you see my whistling arrows strike!" Having tested his men by ordering them to shoot his favorite horse, favorite wife, and his father's favorite horse, he then took aim at his father. Touman died in a hail of arrows. Modun (ruling 209–174 BCE), then "executed his stepmother, his younger brother, and all the high officials of the nation who refused to take orders from him."[14] Having eliminated domestic rivals, his conquest of neighboring northern peoples won over the Xiongnu tribal lords and legitimated his rule.

Han-Xiongnu conflict followed. An attempt at a more pacific relationship was formalized in the *Heqin* (peace through kinship relations) treaty of 198 BCE. The Han sent a royal princess accompanied by substantial quantities of silk, other textiles, and foodstuffs including wine.[15] The Xiongnu thus became the first of the tribute-based nomadic polities. The *Chanyu* would be accorded equal status with the Chinese emperor. In return, the *Chanyu* agreed not to raid China. It was extraordinary that the Chinese emperor, the "Son of Heaven," would consider a leather and felt-clad "barbarian" his equal, but China was hardly in a position of strength. Moreover, such ties, some Chinese officials argued, might indeed tame the "barbarian" and eventually bring him into a properly subordinate relationship.

Royal brides and silk became a common feature of northern nomad-Chinese diplomacy. The princesses complained of their "domed lodgings" with felt walls and diets of horsemeat (still well-represented on Central Asian restaurant menus) and *koumiss* (fermented mare's milk), a continuing favorite of modern Central Asian nomads, who claim that a pint of it has antibiotic properties and all the daily vitamins required for good health. The Emperor Hui dispatched another tearful bride in 192 BCE. Modun aimed higher. In a letter to Hui's mother, the empress Lü, he noted that he was a widower who sought friendship with China and hinted that perhaps he and the widowed Empress could find pleasure in each other's company. The empress demurred, replying that her hair and teeth had fallen out and that the *Chanyu* should not "sully" himself with the likes of her. Meanwhile, Modun, having defeated and driven off the Yuezhi, solidified his hold on the nomads around 176 BCE, informing the Han that he had subjugated "all the people who live by drawing the bow."[16]

The emperor Wendi established border markets for Xiongnu trade and sent a Han bride to Jizhu, Modun's son and successor. Zhonghang Yue, a eunuch and Confucian scholar, accompanied her. He then defected to the Xiongnu and warned his new masters about the fatal allure of Chinese goods. Silk, he declared, was not as useful as leather and felt for nomads, and Chinese foodstuffs were "not as practical or as tasty as milk and koumiss."[17] Statesmen in the nomad camp who had firsthand experience of the sedentary world often expressed the fear that the adoption of too many goods from settled society would deprive the nomads of their martial prowess. Nonetheless, the nomads did make extensive use of silk for clothing, which proved even more useful as a trading commodity. In this way, Chinese silk made its way across Eurasia to Rome.

In 162 BCE, Wendi tried to reaffirm the division of power and sovereignty on both sides of the Great Wall. The peoples north of the Great

Wall, "where men wield the bow and arrow," were subjects of the *Chanyu*, while the peoples south of the Great Wall, who "dwell in houses and wear hats and girdles" (the Chinese), were to be in the domain of the Middle Kingdom. "We and the Chanyu must be as parents to them [all]."[18] Such an arrangement, he argued, would ensure peace. It proved short-lived.

The Xiongnu were consolidating their power in the steppe world with repercussions that reverberated across Eurasia. In 162 BCE, *Chanyu* Jizhu, allied with the Wusun, another (most probably Iranian) nomadic people in the Gansu Corridor, foes of the Yuezhi. He killed the Yuezhi king (making his head into a drinking goblet) and drove them further westward to Afghanistan. The Wusun, with no illusions about their Xiongnu "allies," wisely removed themselves to the Ili river region. The Xiongnu then subjugated the oasis trading cities of the "Western Regions" (Xinjiang), establishing a special administration for this area with its rich agricultural and urban mercantile populations.

Xiongnu conquests sparked a series of westward migrations from the Chinese borderlands. Yuezhi and Iranian nomads rolled across the steppe, ultimately spilling over into Bactria and Iran. The Graeco-Bactrian kingdom was one of the casualties, an event noted by both Chinese and Europeans. Clearly, turbulence in China's northern tribal zone could have ramifications for peoples and states to the west.

China was becoming less secure while the costs of buying off the Xiongnu were mounting. The Han now shifted from *Heqin* diplomacy to confrontation. In 138 BCE, the emperor Wudi (141–87 BCE) sent a special envoy, Zhang Qian, on a secret mission to induce the Yuezhi to join China against the Xiongnu. Zhang was captured by the Xiongnu and spent some ten years with them, gaining intimate knowledge of their society. He eventually escaped with his Xiongnu wife and son and made his way across Central Asia to the now distant Yuezhi. Although he failed to convince the Yuezhi to join in further warfare against the Xiongnu, he made his way back to China, bringing firsthand knowledge of the northern nomads and Central Asia. The Emperor Wudi had already initiated his campaign in 134–3 BCE to subjugate the strategically vital "Western Regions," hoping to deprive the Xiongnu of this important source of tribute, manpower, agricultural, and manufactured products. It would also assure China of easier access to West and South Asia.

Chinese expansion into these dangerous borderlands was justified strategically and economically. Of particular importance to Wudi were the "heavenly" or "blood-sweating" horses of Ferghana. These horses, which were large in comparison with the steppe ponies of the nomads, had this name because of the reddish tinge of their perspiration, probably caused by a parasite on their skin. China needed horses for its army to counter the nomads and to engage in distant military expeditions into Central Asia.

Armed now with Zhang Qian's knowledge, Han campaigns between 127 and 119 BCE penetrated deep into Central Asia. China gained control of the Ordos and sent settlers to secure the region. Han armies took Gansu and advanced as far as Lake Baikal. Mindful of the risks of prolonged warfare in the steppe, China turned to diplomacy and in 115 BCE again dispatched Zhang Qian, the most important intelligence operative of his day. His mission was to win over Central Asian tribes, like the Wusun, to make common cause with China against the Xiongnu. They countered with their own diplomatic measures: the Wusun ruler ended up with both Han and Xiongnu princesses. The Han pressed on, taking Ferghana in 101 BCE. Wudi gained access to the "blood-sweating" horses and scored a major political and psychological point showing that Han power could reach into the nomads' home turf.

China's advances westward, its use of silk for diplomatic and commercial purposes,[19] followed by its securing of Central Asian markets, gave firmer shape to the Silk Road, now a series of intersecting overland trading networks that continued to bring goods across Eurasia. This stabilized the means by which Chinese silk, which had been making its way to Greece and Rome via a complicated series of routes and irregular exchanges since ancient times,[20] now regularly reached the Mediterranean world.

The grueling struggle for control of the "Western Regions," lasting until 60 BCE, produced internal divisions in Xiongnu society. Although sometimes termed a "state," or even an "empire," the Xiongnu realm was first and foremost a tribal confederation. The *Chanyu* was the chief executive officer, combining military, diplomatic, judicial, and even priestly functions. Beneath him were the twenty-four "wise kings" of the left and right and twenty-four other leaders, each in command of 10,000 troops. This "imperial confederation"[21] was flexible and consultative, and it allowed for considerable autonomy in tribal and clan matters.

The *Chanyu's* precedence was most notable in foreign affairs. The Xiongnu tribes, at least in theory, spoke in one voice through him in their dealings with the outside world. In subject sedentary regions, the Xiongnu collected tribute and required labor from the population. Nomads and their herds were subject to an annual census conducted in autumn, but otherwise faced little government interference. The flexibility of nomadic society was both a strength and weakness. It allowed for quick responses to changing situations, but also easily degenerated into factional strife. As long as the central authority provided military and diplomatic success, securing access to the markets of the sedentary world on terms that were favorable to the nomads, the system worked, but disruption of access produced domestic turmoil.

Formerly subject peoples inflicted humiliating losses on the Xiongnu in 72–71 BCE. The Han emperor Xuandi established a Chinese Protectorate of the Western Regions in 60–59 BCE. Prolonged warfare with China had taken its toll, and the Xiongnu were in decline. China encouraged and exploited the growing divisions in Xiongnu society, in particular within the ruling house. The Xiongnu split into two factions: northern and southern. The northern tribes under the *Chanyu* Zhizhi, under pressure from China, moved northward and ultimately westward toward Kangju (the Syr Darya region). China, again risking a campaign deep in the steppe, defeated and killed him. Those tribes that did not drift back remained in Kangju, creating the base for another tribal union that would later move westward toward Europe: the Huns.

Meanwhile, the southern Xiongnu tribes under Zhizhi's brother, the *Chanyu* Huhanye, and remnants of the northern grouping submitted and were rewarded with access to Chinese markets. As the Xiongnu further divided into warring factions, the brilliant Han general Ban Chao unleashed a series of campaigns into Central Asia that reached the Caspian Sea, securing control over this part of the Silk Road. Further attacks in 87–93 CE and 155 CE by nomadic allies of China, the Wuhuan and Xianbei peoples from Manchuria,, who were speakers of early Mongolian,[22] spurred new Xiongnu migrations to the west. The northern confederation now faded. The southern confederation remained on the Chinese borderlands and was drawn into various statelets in the north of China that were created by Xianbei and Qiang (Tibetan) peoples after the fall of the Han in 220. The nomads of the eastern steppes were fragmented and lacked overall leadership.

To the west, two nomad-derived political formations were taking shape: the Kushan Empire and the Huns. In the course of the first centuries BCE and CE, the Kushan dynasty under Kujula Kadphises emerged as the ruling house of the Yuezhi nomads who had overrun the Graeco-Bactrian state. At its height, the Kushan Empire included Bactria, parts of eastern Iran, western and eastern Turkestan, as well as Pakistan (Peshawar served as one of its capitals). Although one of the most powerful and important states of its age, Kushan political history, which has been largely reconstructed from coins and archaeological finds, is murky. Scholars remain divided on the dates of the reigns of the known Kushan rulers. They appear to have reached the apogee of their power sometime in the mid-second century CE, in particular under Kanishka I (ruling, perhaps, about 120–143 CE), possibly a great-grandson of Kujula Kadphises, or Huvishka, who ascended the throne some four years after Kanishka's death and appears to have ruled for thirty-two years. Kanishka, like his ancestor Kujula Kadphises, styled himself "king of kings" and *devaputra*, an Indian title meaning "son of god," an indication that the dynasty was either claiming divine origin or imitating the imperial ideologies of China, India, and Rome.

Sitting astride the crossroads of Central Asia, the Kushan realm displayed a remarkable blending of cultures. Early coins used Greek as their official language, following the traditions of the Graeco-Bactrian kingdom. Later coinage switched to Bactrian, a local East Iranian language, which they wrote using Greek letters. Their coins, usually of gold or copper, have images of Iranian, Indian, and Greek gods on one side and depictions of the ruler on the other. These coins and figurines of various deities found in archaeological sites indicate the coexistence of a broad range of religions: Zoroastrianism, local cults, and Buddhism. Some Kushan rulers patronized and promoted Buddhism, which spread across southern Central Asia to China. Buddhist temples and monasteries were very much a part of the landscape of pre-Islamic Afghanistan.

The art of the Kushan realm combines the realistic representations of the human form typical of Graeco-Roman art with the curvaceous and flowing Indian style and the more formal indigenous Iranian tradition. The Buddha was portrayed wearing a flowing Roman toga. Bodhisattvas (in Buddhist belief, humans who forego entering nirvana and accept reincarnation in order to help humanity and other creatures) were portrayed in the clothing and styles of real people of their time, probably patrons. This sculpture not only continued the earlier Graeco-Bactrian tradition, but also reflected continued contacts with the Graeco-Roman Mediterranean world. Indeed, artisans and artists from the latter made their way to Gandhara (today southeastern Afghanistan and northwestern Pakistan). Some even left their names on the works they created.

The art, especially of the later Kushan period, was largely Buddhist in subject matter. Some works, however, depicted rulers, attired in long coats (often with gold decorations), trousers, and boots that reflected their nomadic heritage. The emphasis is on the expression of power. The Gandharan style later spread to western and eastern Turkestan.

The remains of Kushan monumental art, such as the temple of Surkh Kotal (in Baghlan province, Afghanistan), with its four flights of stairs leading up to a temple devoted to the cult of the heavenly kings, underscore the grandeur of this empire. Inscriptions, often in a variety of languages and scripts, attest to its imperial, universal claims.

Domestically, Kushan kings expanded agriculture through the organization of irrigation projects. As middlemen, they had a significant economic impact on international trade, sending goods by caravan through Central Asia and by sea from Indian ports. They received goods from Egypt, China, and India and were vital to the Silk Road, the fur trade (coming from the Urals), and the commerce in precious stones. Finds of Chinese and Roman goods in the remains of the rulers' palaces give ample evidence of the range of their commercial contacts. As trade and pilgrimage routes often intertwined, the Kushans encouraged Buddhist pilgrimages, promoting international commerce at the same time.

In a process that probably lasted from the 230s to around 270 CE, the Kushan Empire fell to the Sasanids, the newly established rulers of Iran. Sasanid control of this realm was contested in the fourth century CE by new waves of nomads who were called *Hyaona* or *Hyon* in Persian and *Chionitae* in Greek and Latin. Both of these names have been viewed as transcriptions of the same term masked by the Chinese *Xiongnu*. Subsequently, this word appears in Europe as "Hun." Are the Chionitae, Huns, and others bearing similar-sounding names simply the Xiongnu of the Chinese borderlands? Scholars disagree on this matter. The most recent studies argue for a connection.[23] The rise and fall of the Xiongnu had pushed various nomadic peoples, in particular Turkic groupings, away from the Chinese and Mongolian borderlands and brought them westward to the Kazakh steppes. What seems most likely is that a tribal union containing some core elements associated with the original Xiongnu and continuing to bear this very prestigious name among the steppe nomads, made its way into Kazakhstan. In the Kazakh steppes, additional tribes joined, forming a new tribal union: the Huns.

In 375 CE, perhaps again under pressure from tribal movements in Central Asia, these "Huns" crossed the Volga River, smashing the Alans, a powerful Iranian people residing in the Caspian-Pontic steppes since the first century CE (the Osetins of Caucasia are their descendants) and their neighbors, the Gothic tribal unions. These dislocations contributed to waves of migrations in which the mainly Germanic tribes of the Roman borderlands pushed into a crumbling Roman defense system. The Hun raids, much like those that had struck China, harassed the Roman borderlands. In the 440s, Attila, a Hunnic chieftain, took power over a large grouping of Huns and subject Germanic, Slavic, and other peoples in Pannonia (Hungary) and adjoining lands. He plundered Roman lands, seeking loot and tribute, not territorial conquests. The Roman Empire, however feeble it may have been due to internal discord, was never really in danger from him. When Attila died at his wedding feast in 453 CE, perhaps poisoned by his bride, his confederation quickly collapsed. The Huns melted back into the steppe, occasionally appearing as Roman mercenaries.

The Xiongnu collapse had sent the first wave of nomads westward. Europe's first close encounter with Central Asian nomads left a lasting memory and a legend far out of proportion to its actual impact. The Huns became symbols of the unbridled barbarian. Despite their ferocious reputations, the Huns, east and west, were never a threat to the existence of China or the Roman Empire.

CHAPTER THREE

Heavenly Qaghans: The Türks and Their Successors

fter a period of political instability following the collapse of the Xiongnu and Han, three important states emerged: the Tabghach (Chinese: Tuoba) in northern China, the Asian Avars (Chinese: Hua and Rouran) in Mongolia, and more distantly the Hephthalites in the Kushan lands. The Tabghach, who took the Chinese dynastic name Northern Wei (386–534), controlled all of China north of the Yellow River, Xinjiang, and part of the steppe zone by 439. Their capital, Pingcheng (near modern Datong), was within reach of the steppes, the primary source of their 100,000 soldiers and reputedly one million horses.

The Wei elite, perhaps 20 percent of whom were Tabghach, comprised 119 clans and tribal groups as well as Chinese, the majority of their subjects. A governing minority, the Tabghach employed older Xianbei models of separate administrations for Chinese and tribal peoples. Nonetheless, the attractions of Chinese culture proved irresistible to the elite, who adopted Chinese speech, clothing, food, and court culture. In the late fifth century, the half-Chinese emperor Xiao Wen-ti banned the Tabghach language,[1] personal names, and clothing at court. He took a new Chinese family name, Yuan, and moved the capital to Luoyang in the southern, more Chinese part of their state.

The Tabghach maintained some distinctions through religion, actively promoting Buddhism, then a foreign faith in China, which had come to Han China from the Kushans via the Silk Road. Tabghach interest in Buddhism grew as their commercial relations with Central Asia deepened by the last quarter of the fifth century.

Asian Avar affiliations remains obscure. According to the Wei dynastic annals, their ruling house descended from an early fourth-century Wei slave. His master called him Mugulü, "head has become bald," an ironic reference to his hair-line which began at his eyebrows. Mugulü fled to the steppe, where he gathered a band of some 100 fellow escapees and desperados. His son, Juluhui, completed the transformation of what was probably little more than a robber band into a people, acknowledged Wei overlordship, and sent an annual tribute of horses, cattle, and furs. This gained him access to Chinese markets. With Juluhui a pattern of political confederation emerges: the development of a people, often very rapidly, from a band of warriors led by a charismatic chieftain. The fifth-century Avar ruler Shelun took the Xianbei title *Qaghan*, a term of unknown origin, which denoted "emperor" in the steppe.

Juluhui adopted the sobriquet *Rouran*, which Chinese accounts transferred to his followers, later mockingly changing it to *Ruanruan* (wriggling insects). The Rouran called themselves *Abar* or *Avar*. A formidable military power, their conquests produced a realm extending from the Gobi Desert to Lake Baikal, and from Xinjiang to Manchuria and the borders of modern Korea. Chinese accounts credited Avar shamans with the ability to summon snowstorms to conceal their retreats following a defeat. Weather magic was attributed to many Turko-Mongolian peoples.

The Hephthalites emerged in the old Kushan lands out of various "Hunnic" groupings that left the Altai around 350–370. In the mid-fifth century, they came under the leadership of the Hephthal dynasty.[2] Controlling Sogdia, much of Xinjiang, and northern India, these troublesome "Huns" of the Persian borderlands figured in Sasanid affairs, saving or ending the careers of several shahs. They built on Graeco-Bactrian and Kushan traditions, adopted the Bactrian language, and developed an interest in Buddhism, Zoroastrianism, Hinduism, and various Indo-Iranian gods. To this mix, they added Christianity and Manichaeism, a new arrival in Central Asia. Its Iranian founder, Mani (216–277), came from Mesopotamia, an area rich in religious ideas. He saw himself as the culmination of the prophetic traditions of Zoroaster, Buddha, and Jesus.

Manichaeism combined aspects of all of these religions, everywhere adjusting its profile to suit local sensibilities. Nonetheless, most governments distrusted its otherworldliness and persecuted its followers. Manichaeans viewed the world as engulfed in a conflict between Evil, represented by matter and Good, a spiritual plane represented by light. Their purpose was to release the light/spirit from matter, by leading ascetic lives and avoiding as much as possible material-physical temptations. The clergy or "elect," fully initiated into the mysteries of the faith, led lives of poverty and chastity. The mass of believers, the "listeners," supported them.

Hephthalite customs struck outsiders as unusual. Brothers shared a common wife. Wives placed horns on their headdress to indicate the number of their husbands. The head-binding of infants produced deformed, elongated skulls. Deliberate cranial deformation was widespread among some steppe peoples. The practice may have produced seizures in some individuals, which were akin to the hallucinatory trances of shamans.

These three states sent ripple effects across Eurasia. Avar-Wei wars drove tribes westward. These and earlier migrations transformed the steppes from what had been an area of Iranian speech into one that was increasingly Turkic. Among the peoples who came to the Black Sea steppes, around 460, were Oghur Turkic tribes,[3] part of a loose union called *Tiele* in Chinese, which sprawled across Eurasia. The Avar qaghan, Anagui (520–552), facing eastern Tiele unrest and internal foes, turned to the Wei for help, but they had split into rival eastern and western branches. These political crises provided the backdrop to the rise of the Türk[4] Empire.

Little is really known about the origins of the Türks. Their ruling clan bore the name *Ashina*, probably an eastern Iranian or Tokharian word (*ashsheina* or *ashna*) meaning "blue,"[5] which can denote the east in the Turkic system, borrowed from China, of associating colors with compass points. According to Chinese renderings of Türk legends, the Ashina Türks descended from the mating of a she-wolf and the sole survivor of a tribe annihilated by enemies.[6] The theme of a ruling clan born of a wolf or suckled by a wolf is widespread across Eurasia.[7] The Chinese accounts place the Ashina in Gansu and Xinjiang, areas associated with Iranian and Tokhharian peoples. This legacy may account for important eastern Iranian elements in the early Türk union. From this region they migrated in the fifth century to the Altai Mountains, with its Turkic-speaking inhabitants, where they became subject ironsmiths of the Avars.

The ambitious ruler of the Türks, Bumïn, after helping his overlord to suppress a Tiele revolt in 546, requested an Avar bride in 551. The Avars haughtily refused. The western Wei, with whom Bumïn had drawn close, immediately granted Bumïn a royal princess and he destroyed the Avar Empire in 552. Anagui committed suicide, and by 555 the Avars ceased to be a factor in the eastern steppes.

Bumïn, whose name, like those of many early Türk rulers, is not Turkic, assumed the title of *Qaghan*, but soon died. His sons Keluo and Mughan and his brother Ishtemi subjugated the tribes and statelets north of China and forged an empire from Manchuria to the Black Sea. This was the first trans-Eurasian state directly linking Europe with East Asia. The eastern European-western Central Asian conquests were the work of Ishtemi, also known as the *Sir Yabghu Qaghan* (a title just below that of the Qaghan). *Sir* derives from Sanskrit *Śrî* (fortunate, auspicious), and *Yabghu* may be Iranian. These titles show the wide range of non-Turkic influences in the shaping of Türk imperial culture.

Allied with Sasanid Iran, Ishtemi crushed the Hephthalites, most probably between 557 and 563. The Türks, having taken Transoxiana (the land beyond the Oxus River), including Sogdia, burst into the Black Sea steppes, seeking their fugitive "slaves," the Avars. By the 560s, the Byzantines report contact with a people migrating from the east who called themselves Avars, but whom some Byzantines considered "Pseudo-Avars."[8] Whether they were the remnants of the Asian Avars or some people who used their name remains a matter of controversy. Whatever their origins, they were soon caught up in the conflicting political and commercial interests of the Türk, Sasanid, and Byzantine empires.

In Central Asia, silk played a key role in diplomacy and functioned as an international currency. The extraction of silk from China not only brought wealth, but also legitimated a ruler's sovereignty. Silk was big business and had political consequences. The Sasanids and Sogdians were the principal middlemen in moving the cargoes of the Silk Road from Central Asia to the Mediterranean world. Sogdian colonies along the Silk Road extended to Inner Mongolia and China. Coached by their Sogdian vassals, the skilled money managers and traders of East-West commerce, the Türks, had become major traffickers in silk. Chinese accounts attributed Türk success to their Sogdian advisers, whom they viewed as "malicious and crafty."[9] Given the close Türko-Sogdian cooperation, a Türk-Sasanid alliance was untenable.

In 568, a major Türk embassy, mainly staffed by Sogdians, came to Constantinople seeking to establish ongoing commercial relations and to end Byzantine "appeasement" of their fugitive "slaves," the Avars. According to Byzantine accounts, Ishtemi was determined that the Avars, who, he declared, were neither birds who can fly nor fish who can "hide in the depths of the sea," would not escape Türk swords.[10] Meanwhile, the "European Avars" retreated to Pannonia (modern Hungary), Attila's earlier base. From the Hungarian steppes, they caused considerable turmoil in the Balkans, raiding (often together with the Slavs) and extorting hefty tributes from the Byzantines until the Franks of Charlemagne destroyed their state in the last decade of the eighth century.

The Türks offered Constantinople an alliance against Iran, silk, and even iron. Byzantium agreed, but remained cautious about war with Iran and preferred to buy off the Avars. Byzantine emissaries traveled across Central Asia (perhaps as far as present day Kyrgyzstan) for audiences with Türk rulers. In the first Byzantine embassy, after 568, the ambassador Zemarchus was bedazzled by Ishtemi, living in silk-bedecked tents, perched alternately upon a golden throne mounted on two wheels (so that it could be moved by horse), and various gold couches, including one resting on four golden peacocks. Relations were uneasy. At a subsequent embassy in 576, Tardu, Ishtemi's successor, greeted Valentinus, the Byzantine ambassador, in anger, venting his rage at Constantinople's failure to attack Iran and berating the Byzantines for "speaking with ten tongues" and lying with all of them.[11]

Internal Türk politics were complex. The qaghanate was administratively divided into eastern and western halves, each ruled by an Ashina qaghan. The eastern qaghan was politically senior. This dual kingship, while providing flexibility in managing local affairs, also produced rivalries. Ishtemi's successors occasionally tried to seize power in the east. Such attempts were "legal" because, as in most Central Asian nomadic states, any member of the royal clan had the right to claim supreme power. Seeking to forestall family strife, the Türks created a system of succession in which younger brothers were to succeed older brothers and then sons of the oldest brother would succeed the youngest uncle and so on. Many were impatient, resulting in throne struggles that sapped the strength of the state. Attempts to create workable succession systems bedeviled virtually all Central Asian nomadic states.

While Ishtemi was establishing Türk power in the west, the eastern Türks were exploiting the rivalries of China's Northern Qi (550–577) and Northern Zhou (557–581) dynasties, acquiring royal brides and silk in exchange for peace. Tatpar Qaghan, while professing surprise that his "two loyal sons to the south"[12] were feuding, manipulated a divided China to enrich his realm.

The Sui dynasty (581–618) seized power and reunited China. The Sui, ethnically Chinese, had intimate familiarity with the northern non-Chinese regimes and the steppe. They immediately set about strengthening their northern defenses while Chinese operatives such as Zhengsun Sheng carefully cultivated agents at the Türk court and encouraged strife among the Ashina. While fissures among the eastern Türks deepened, the western Türk qaghan, Tardu, made a bid for power over east and west, achieving his goal for a few years until a revolt of the Tiele, perhaps encouraged by the Sui, ended his imperial dreams in 603.

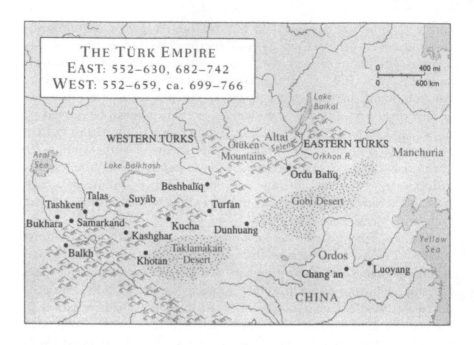

THE TÜRK EMPIRE
EAST: 552–630, 682–742
WEST: 552–659, ca. 699–766

Tong Yabghu (618–630) restored western Türk qaghanal authority, extended his rule to southern Afghanistan, and played a major role in Byzantium's 628 victory over Sasanid Iran in a war that enveloped the Middle East and Transcaucasia. At home, however, his harsh rule led to his assassination and civil war. The western Türks emerged from the chaos divided into two tribal unions, collectively termed the *On Oq* (Ten Arrows), each led by its own qaghan.

Around 630, the Chinese Buddhist monk/traveler Xuanzang, on his way to India visited Tong Yabghu's court at Suyâb. His report confirms the picture of spectacular wealth noted in the Byzantine accounts. The qaghan "was covered with a robe of green satin" and bound his loose hair "with a silken band some ten feet in length." The "200 officers" of his entourage were attired in "brocade stuff," and accompanying "troops" were "clothed in furs and fine spun hair garments." Astride their camels and horses, they were armed with "lances and bows and standards. The eye could not estimate their number."[13] The qaghan's tent was "adorned with golden flower ornaments which blind the eye with their glitter." His "officers," all "clad in shining garments of embroidered silk," sat on long mats, in two rows before him while his guard corps "stood behind them." Xuanzang was impressed that this "ruler of a wandering horde" had a "certain dignified arrangement about his surroundings."[14] The qaghan ordered wine and music for his guests to accompany a sumptuous meal of mutton and chicken. Among the things that particularly struck Xuanzang was a nature preserve that the qaghan kept to the west of Suyâb which held herds of deer, each wearing bells and accustomed to human contact. Anyone who dared to kill these deer would be executed.[15]

Meanwhile, momentous changes occurred in the east. China's attempts to conquer Vietnam and Koguryo, a state straddling Korea and Manchuria, were costly and produced rebellions. The eastern Türks aided the rebels. The Tang (618–907) toppled the fading Sui and ushered in one of China's most brilliant periods. Facing continual raids from the eastern Türk qaghan, Xieli, the Tang bought him off with goods, while covertly promoting intra-Ashina feuding and rebellions. Even the elements seemed to be conspiring against Xieli; several years of severe snows and frosts had produced famine in the steppe. People fled his harsh taxes and bad luck. The Tang captured him and he died in captivity in 630.

The eastern qaghanate had fallen and perhaps as many as one million bedraggled nomads surrendered. They were settled on China's northern frontiers. Türk chieftains received Chinese titles and offices. The higher aristocracy came to the Tang court where a number of them went on to successful military careers. According to Chinese accounts, the various chieftains of the northern tribes asked the Tang Emperor Taizong to take the title of *Tian Kehan* (Turkic: *Tengri Qaghan*), "Heavenly Qaghan," in imitation of a steppe ruler. Taizong declared that he alone "loved" the nomads, and as a consequence they followed him "like a father or mother."[16] It was an extraordinary claim by the Tang, made all the more extraordinary by the apparent willingness of the northern nomads to accept it.

China now fully asserted its power in Central Asia. In 640, Taizong conquered Kocho, a city on the Silk Road in Xinjiang in the western Türk orbit with a long history of close ties to China. Other city-states soon submitted. The cultural impact of these sophisticated trading cities on the already cosmopolitan Tang court was considerable. Central Asian music (rulers often sent "gifts" of musicians), instruments, dance, along with performers from the "Western Regions," especially Sogdia and Kucha, artists, and art styles all became fashionable in the Chinese capital. The emperor Xuanzong, who kept 30,000 musicians, even learned to play the Kuchean "wether drum," and his infamous concubine, Yang Guifei, loved Sogdian dances which were famous for their leaps and whirls. Some court officials were offended by the Sogdian dance "Sprinkling Cold Water on the Barbarian" which, apparently, involved nude performers and the splashing around of mud and water. It was banned in 713.

Nonetheless, Sogdian entertainers, including dancers, jugglers, and acrobats, remained popular along with clothing fashions and various fabrics from Central Asia. All of this came to Chang'an and Luoyang, the Tang capitals, together with foodstuffs, exotic plants, animals (such as peacocks), wines, utensils, precious stones, and works of art. This commercial web extended far to the west and included goods from Iran and Byzantium. Central Asian cities were not only intermediaries in this trade, but also active producers, especially of textiles and exporters of special foods such as melons and the "golden peaches of Samarkand."

By 659, the fragmented western Türks had submitted to an advancing China. For a time, Chinese hegemony extended to parts of Afghanistan and the borders of Iran. The costs of empire were expensive and not without competition. The Tibetans had begun to make their presence felt in Xinjiang in the 660s and 670s, driving the Chinese from some of their holdings in the Tarim Basin. They held much of the region for several decades and for a time threatened to become the dominant power.[17]

Revolts in the western and eastern Türk regions further weakened the Tang presence. The early eighth-century Türkic runic inscriptions on large steles, part of the burial complexes of the rulers, located in the Türk core territory on the Orkhon River in Mongolia recount the epic drama of the revival of the Türk Empire. In the inscriptions, the deceased directly addresses the people. The inscription erected around 726 and dedicated to Tonyuquq, the Chinese-educated chief adviser of the early qaghans of the second Türk Empire, depicts the sorry state of the Türks, a leaderless, subject people: "Tengri ["heaven," the supreme Türk celestial deity] must have spoken thus: 'I gave you a khan, you left the khan and again became subjects.' Because you became subjects, Tengri must have said 'die!' The Türk people perished, were destroyed, became nothing."[18]

Tonyuquq then tells how a small band of 700 men hiding out in the hills, some on horseback, others on foot, became an army that restored the empire for the new qaghan, Ilterish, by 682. Tonyuquq, who clearly relished his role as kingmaker, adds, "because Tengri gave me wisdom, I myself made him [Ilterish] Qaghan."[19] In their monuments, Ilterish's sons, Bilge Qaghan and his brother and chief adviser, Kül Tegin, chastise the Türks for succumbing to the "sweet words" and alluring "gold, silver, and silken goods" of China and for abandoning the ways of their ancestors. According to them, Ilterish, began with only seventeen warriors, but "was like a wolf" and his "enemies were like sheep."[20] Ilterish's brother and successor, Qapaghan Qaghan (691–716), restored the empire to its earlier glory.

The Türk state apparatus, offices, and titles, many of Chinese, Sogdian, Tokharian, and Indian origins, were largely inherited from the Rouran. The qaghan claimed that he was "heaven-like, heaven-conceived" and possessed *qut* (heavenly good fortune), a sign of the heavenly mandate to rule. His person was holy and his blood could not be shed. If a qaghan had to be removed—permanently—he was strangled with a silk cord. His investiture ceremony included ritual strangulation in which, on the point of losing consciousness, clearly an induced journey into the spirit world, he was asked to state the length of his rule. Possession of the holy Ötüken Highlands and sacred grounds along the Orkhon River confirmed the qaghan's political legitimacy. The ideology of *qut* was similar to the Chinese concept that the emperor was the "son of heaven" and ruled by divine favor. It is not clear whether this similarity was a borrowing from one to the other or simply part of a common pool of ideological resources.

The Türks, like many of their subjects, were believers in *Tengri*. They also worshipped *Umay*, a goddess associated with fertility, and *Yol Tengri*, a god of the road (or fate). In addition, there were cults of earth-water, holy mountains, and forests. They venerated their ancestors, annually conducting special ceremonies at the ancestral cave from which they believed the Ashina had sprung. Contact with other civilizations introduced new religions—usually brought in by the Sogdians. Tatpar became interested in Buddhism. He read Turkic translations of Buddhist tracts and ordered the building of a Buddhist temple. The nomad leadership opposed it. Bilge Qaghan also considered building Taoist and Buddhist temples. Tonyuquq dissuaded him from doing so, arguing, as others had before him, that Türk power derived from their nomadic lifestyle. Permanent structures threatened their martial vigor; the Türk "capital" was wherever the qaghan's cart stopped or his tent was pitched. Temples were not portable.

Pastoral nomadism remained a mainstay of the Türk economy and horsepower remained the key to their military might. Highly mobile armies gave them control of the trans-Eurasian trade routes. They collected revenue from trade, tribute, agricultural, and manufactured products from subject tribes and city-states. Raiding was another source of income. The redistribution of wealth was one of the principal means that nomadic rulers had to maintain their power among the tribes. A qaghan was "loved" and respected only as long as he kept his military followers well-fed and clothed and provided opportunities for their enrichment.

The Türks grew wealthy, but the costs of maintaining a far-flung, ethnically diverse empire were great. The harsh Türk regime had to expend much energy on punitive missions against ever-rebellious tribes. Qapaghan perished in one such campaign. Internal discord persisted. Rivals poisoned Ilterish's son, Bilge Qaghan in 734. External threats were not lacking. The Arabs after their conquest of Iran in 651 challenged western Türk dominance in Sogdia in the early eighth century, weakening their control of the Silk Road.

In 742, the Basmïl (led by a branch of the Ashina), heading a coalition of subject tribes, overthrew the Türks. The Uighurs then toppled the Basmïl in 744. The resultant Uighur qaghanate (744–840), centered in Mongolia and Xinjiang, with extensions into Siberia, exploited Tang difficulties. The Uighurs, numbering perhaps 800,000, led a tribal confederation called Toquz Oghuz, meaning "the nine related groups" of eastern Tiele origin. In a 759 inscription honoring the founder of the state, Qutlugh Bilge Kül Qaghan, he boasts to his people that the conquered Türks "thereafter ceased to exist." Calling upon "the common people," whom he left unmolested, to join him, the Uighur ruler drove off potential rivals, pursued the "sinful nobles" and "carried off their livestock, movable possessions, unmarried girls, and widows."[21]

In 755, An Lushan, a Tang general of Sogdian and Türkic descent, allegedly the lover of the emperor's concubine, revolted against his overlord. Rebellions continued even after An Lushan's assassination two years later. The Tang turned to the Uighurs for help. They happily complied, defeated the rebels, and were allowed to sack the royal capitals as a reward. The Uighurs supported the Tang in order to better exploit China, extorting great quantities of silk and other goods under the guise of gift-giving and trade. In return for the silk, the Uighurs sent horses, many of them infirm or moribund. The Tang, understandably, were often late in their payments.

This policy was the work of Bögü Qaghan, whose mother was a Tang princess. In 762, Sogdian Manichaeans converted him to their faith. Sizable numbers of Sogdians in China appear to have supported the An Lushan revolt. Their search for a protector in China against an anti-foreign backlash might explain their interest in converting Bögü. His reasons remain obscure. The Uighur elite adopted Manichaeism. They believed, perhaps, that in addition to spiritual benefits there were political, economic, cultural, and social advantages to be gained by conversion, even though the bearers of the new religion were nowhere a politically dominant group. Perhaps the Uighurs were looking for a religion that came with no political encumbrances.

Important Uighur factions opposed the overweening Sogdian influence. Tun Bagha Tarqan, Bögü Qaghan's uncle, an opponent of the new religion and the aggressive China policy, urged on the qaghan by his Sogdian advisors, led a palace coup. Bögü Qaghan perished, but Manichaeism survived.

Unlike the Türks, the Uighurs built cities—with the assistance of the Sogdians and Chinese. They established their capital, Ordu Balïq, on the Orkhon River in 757. Tamîm ibn Bahr, an Arab visitor to the capital in the early ninth century, was impressed with the size, wealth, and power of the Uighur Empire. The qaghan had a personal army of 12,000 and his seventeen subordinate chieftains each commanded armies of 13,000. This was an imposing force, including women warriors such as the "seven women archers skillful on horseback"[22] whom the Uighurs sent to the Tang.

No less impressive was the capital, fortified with a series of walls. The qaghan's palace had its own wall, as did the city center, which contained temples as well as administrative offices. The outer wall had twelve large iron gates leading into busy market streets filled with merchants hawking their goods and services such as ceramics and stone carving. Purveyors of the same products were usually grouped together on the same streets, as was typical of many medieval cities. There were high towers to watch for invaders coming from the surrounding steppes. Nomadic traditions, however, remained. The Uighur qaghan had a tent made of gold which stood atop his castle and could be seen from miles away. The tent could accommodate one hundred people. In contrast to many nomad-founded "cities" in the steppe, which were little more than short-lived conglomerations of tents with a section containing a few mud-baked buildings, this was a real city.[23]

Medieval travelers occasionally encountered the ruins of abandoned steppe cities. Tamîm ibn Bahr passed by one such site, near Lake Issyk Kul. He reports that he saw "traces of an ancient town," but none of the local Turks knew who had built it and why it had become deserted. Recent discoveries of a Uighur palace complex at Khökh Ordung (Blue Palace, in the eastern foothills of the Khangai Mountains in Mongolia), dating from the late sixth to the early seventh century, shed new light on the history of Uighur urban development. This city, built of white brick and pink-tinted gray roof tiles, resembled a nomadic encampment. Its centerpiece, the qaghan's pavilion, imitated a tent on a grand scale. Kökh Ordung, meant to awe outsiders, indicated Uighur imperial ambitions well before their victory of 744. It was also the site of some kind of daily sun-worship by the ruler.[24] Another example of Uighur imperial grandeur was Bezeklik (literally "the place with paintings"). Consisting of seventy-seven artificially created caves, dating from the fifth to ninth centuries, the paintings within depict Buddhist and Manichaean themes, in a mix of Sogdian, Chinese, and Indian styles. Because of the richness of its finds, scholars have called it "the Pompeii of the Desert."

The image of these eighth- or ninth-century Uighur princesses, elaborately coifed and beautifully attired in silk robes, is preserved in the Bezeklik "Thousand Buddha Caves" near the site of Gaochang, an oasis city near modern Turfan in Xinjiang. In some respects Bezeklik, a major Uighur center containing Manichaean and Buddhist art and culture, is akin to Dunhuang, the Buddhist temple-cave cultural complex located in Gansu province in China. Bildarchiv Preussischer Kulturbesitz / Art Resource, New York

The first half of the ninth century was a tumultuous era. China was in decline. Tibet, hitherto a major regional power, after 842 collapsed in civil war between competing pro- and anti-Buddhist factions. The Tibetans retreated from Central Asia and would never again be an important military power. The Uighurs faced factional power struggles and wars against the Tibetans, Qarluqs, and Kyrgyz, a powerful Turkic or Turkicized tribal union centered in the Yenisei region of Tuva. The Kyrgyz, pouncing on the Uighurs weakened by throne struggles, disease, and famine in the steppe, overran the capital in 840. A Kyrgyz gravestone commemorating Tirig Beg, one of the participants in this victory, describes him as "like a sharp-tusked wild boar" who killed twenty-two enemies.[25] Weighed down by wealth and tied to their cities, the Uighurs were easy prey.

Some Uighur tribes fled to the Chinese borderlands and subsequently formed a series of small states in Xinjiang and Gansu. They mixed with and ultimately Turkicized the local eastern Iranian and Tokharian populations. The Uighurs, hitherto predominantly nomad pastoralists, began to settle, taking up urban and agricultural pursuits. Like their mentors, the Sogdians, they developed a rich commercial culture as Silk Road traders and a complex spiritual life in which Manichaeism, Buddhism, and Christianity were all represented. In the eastern steppe zone, they replaced the Sogdians as culture-bearers. The Aramaeo-Syriac script (related to the Hebrew and Arabic alphabets), which the Sogdians had adopted in various forms to write their language, was also used to write Uighur. From the Uighurs it passed to the Mongols and is still used by the Mongols of Inner Mongolia. The Manchus borrowed it from the Mongols. The post-imperial Uighurs produced a rich literature, largely religious in content, for a population of which perhaps one-third was literate. The shift in the role of the Uighurs is reflected in a phrase from an early tenth-century Arab historian, Ibn al-Faqîh, who called them "the Arabs of the Turks."[26]

The Kyrgyz who replaced them stemmed from a complex society of nomads and agriculturalists, but were not as culturally sophisticated as the Uighurs. Their early history remains murky, as does their "imperial era" from 840 to the early tenth century. Breaking with traditions that dated back to the Xiongnu, they did not center their state on the Orkhon and Selenge rivers nor attempt wider conquests. Instead, they returned to their native Yenisei, from where they maintained commercial contact with China and the Middle East. Muslim geographers knew them as livestock breeders and a source of goods from the Siberian forests, such

This traveling monk is depicted in the art of the Mogao Caves of Dunhuang, also called "Caves of the Thousand Buddhas." These man-made caves, begun in the fourth century CE, *housed almost 500 temples. This religious and cultural complex, full of artworks and manuscripts, was China's entry point onto the Silk Road. Monks followed the trading routes as they made their pilgrimages across Central Asia.* British Museum / Art Resource, New York as musk, furs, special types of wood, and the *khutu* horn, apparently mammoth tusks which they dug up—a source of ivory.

The Qitan, a Mongolic people, filled the apparent power vacuum in Mongolia. They were a powerful tribal union of hunters, trappers, pig-raising agriculturalists, and sheep and horse breeders from southern Manchuria. Former subjects of the Türks, they created an empire (916–1125) in northern China and Manchuria, adopting the Chinese dynastic name of Liao. Having taken Mongolia, they invited the Uighurs, who once reigned there, to return. The Uighurs politely declined. The Qitan garrisoned Mongolia, but focused on China. Their harsh rule and onerous taxes induced many Turkic groupings to migrate. During the tenth and eleventh centuries, the demographic balance in Mongolia tilted in favor of Mongolic-speakers. Mongolia became Mongolian, but Qitan rulers preferred to be Chinese Emperors.

The Türks created the first Central Asian transcontinental empire, from Manchuria to the Black Sea, promoting an extensive trade network that facilitated the movement of goods and ideas. It would be almost 500 years before another empire would similarly unite the steppes. The age of "Heaven-conceived Qaghans" had ended—for a time—but left a model of governance dating back to the Xiongnu. It became the template for nomad successor states, large and small.

CHAPTER FOUR

The Cities of the Silk Road and the Coming of Islam

O n the eve of the Arab invasions of Transoxiana in the seventh and eighth centuries, there were a series of oasis city-states that formed links in the northern Silk Road. Khwarazm, an agricultural, manufacturing, and trading center west of the Sogdian cities of Châch (Tashkent), Bukhara, and Samarkand, was a major conduit to the Middle East for the goods of the Finno-Ugrian and Slavic peoples of the northern forests. Al-Muqaddasî, an Arab geographer writing around 985, enumerates an extraordinary range of goods imported from Khwarazm: "sable, squirrel, ermine, weasel, marten, fox and beaver hides, rabbit skins of various colors, goat skins, wax, arrows, hats, fish glue, fish teeth, castor, amber, honey, hazelnuts, falcons, swords, armor, *khalanj* [birch wood], slaves, sheep and cattle."[1]

The Sogdians, farmers, handicraftsmen, and merchants, with trading colonies dotting Eurasia from China to the Crimea, dominated this commercial world, providing the technical and financial expertise. Traces of their presence have been found from Japan to Belgium. Some of their caravans crossed substantial parts of Eurasia; others simply delivered local goods from one town to the next. No job was too big or too small. Archaeological finds, scattered fragments of correspondence, and Arab narratives of their conquests have only recently allowed scholars to gain some insight into the internal workings of the Sogdians and their southern neighbors in Bactria. Sogdian traders often formed family companies with representatives in major cities and smaller settlements. Sogdians in China also became government officials, army officers, farmers and horse breeders. Communal leaders, called *sartapao* (Chinese: *sabao*), a word borrowed from Sanskrit *sârthavâha* (caravan-chief), emerged.[2] This word alone shows the polyglot, international character of their connections.

The Sogdian "Ancient Letters," from fourth century CE merchants in Gansu to their home bases in Sogdia, provide fragmentary but occasionally graphic descriptions of daily life, personal concerns, and contemporary events. One letter from a daughter to her mother tells of her difficulty in returning home since her husband's family, apparently, would not allow it.

The woman complains of her wretchedness and poverty. Only a "priest" helps her and is willing to give her a camel and a man to accompany her, but she seems to need a letter from her mother. Another woman, named Miwnay, writes to her husband Nanai-dhat, who apparently abandoned her, that she would rather be married to a dog or a pig than to be his wife.[3]

Tang artists produced accurate figurines of the Sogdians and other non-Han peoples carrying out their daily pursuits. Sogdians in what is today Xinjiang farmed and were engaged in a variety of crafts, including "nailers of camels' feet." As long- and short-distance traders, they were, by necessity, experts in camel handling. Réunion des Musées Nationaux / Art Resource, New York

South of Sogdia lay Bactria, earlier under Kushan and Hephthalite rule, a major center of Zoroastrianism and Buddhism. Xuanzang reports that it had "100 convents and 3000 monks."[4] Statues of the Buddha were adorned with gold and gems—an attraction for raiders as well as the faithful. According to legend, Alexander the Great built its principal city, Baktra (later Balkh). Less urbanized than Sogdia, Bactria with its castles and villages resembled neighboring Sasanid Iran. The Iranian Bactrian language, mainly written in Greek script, had loanwords from Semitic languages, Greek, Sanskrit, Sasanid Persian, Chinese, and Turkic, reflecting its complex cultural history.

To the east, in Xinjiang, there was another series of oasis city-states or kingdoms clustered in the Tarim Basin and Turfan region in the north and Khotan in the south. Caught between the nomadic powers in the steppes and China they had often enjoyed an uneasy independence or autonomy since Han times. In the seventh century, China and Tibet contested the region. China organized Kashghar, Agni (today Qarashahr), Kucha, and Khotan into the "Four Garrisons of the Anxi Protectorate" (*Anxi* means "pacify the west") and uneasily held sway here until 751.

Regionally, Khotan dominated the south and Kashghar the west. Khotanese legends trace the city's origins to the milieu of Ashoka, the Indian ruler who adopted Buddhism in the third century BCE. Indian-Buddhist influences remained strong and Indians were the second-largest grouping of the population, after the Iranian Saka. Khotan was a center for white and green jade and silk. According to local legends depicted on murals, the silk worms were smuggled into Khotan in the elaborate coiffure of a second century CE Chinese princess (other accounts say she was a princess from Kucha) who had been sent to marry the Khotanese ruler.[5] Xuanzang, who records this tale, reports that Khotan's inhabitants were urbane Buddhists with a love of music and dance. They also had some unusual practices. For instance, they had built a temple to make offerings to the local rats, large silver or golden-colored beasts. According to local lore, the Khotanese king, faced with a "Xiongnu" attack, appealed to the rats for aid against the invaders, who were camped on the rat mounds outside the city. A giant rat appeared to the King in a dream and agreed to help. The rats then chewed through the leather armor, horse gear, and bowstrings of the Xiongnu, guaranteeing a victory for the Khotanese.[6] A painting of what a British traveler called a "rat-headed divinity" was taken from the area and is now found in the collections of the British Museum.[7]

Kucha, Agni, and Qocho were substantial city-states inhabited by peoples who spoke Tokharian until at least the eighth century. Their economy combined agriculture, livestock breeding, and handicrafts production. They exported foodstuffs, wine, silk, textiles, felt, jade, and cosmetics. The whole of this region experienced profound cultural influences from China and India. The range of languages and scripts used in these crossroads of Eurasia was extraordinary. Documents and inscriptions have been found in Chinese, Tibetan, Turkic, Tokharian, Indic, Greek, Armenian, various Semitic, Iranian, and lesser-known languages.

In Transoxiana, the Türks were the dominant power until 650, although their rule was sometimes indirect. Of the local city-states, only Khwarazm, under its king the *Khwârazmshâh*, had a centralized state. The Sogdians formed a more decentralized union. Bukhara and Samarkand shared a common royal house: the Jamûg.[8] The "Lord of Bukhara" had a camel-shaped throne, surely a reference to the importance of the caravan trade to their economy. Occasionally, accounts mention a "King of Sogdia," who, at best, was a "first among equals." Although rulers enjoyed little real power, the *History of Bukhara*, written by Narshahkî in the 940s, describes a royal court rich in pomp and ceremony. In the early eighth century, just prior to the Arab conquest, the *Khâtûn* (queen), mother of the underage "Lord of Bukhara," Tughshâda, governed. She held court sitting on her throne while slaves, eunuchs, and nobles gathered before her. Two hundred "youths girded with gold belts and swords carried (on the shoulder)" daily came from the countryside to serve her. She dispensed justice in the morning, went to her castle for lunch (sending trays of food to her "entire retinue"), and then resumed her court in the afternoon until sunset.[9]

Narshakhî claims that Bukhara had 1000 shops, among which he notes the "green grocers' stalls" next to the city walls and the "pistachio shellers" who were near them. The "spice sellers" were in yet another region and a gate was named after them. Walls separated the city's districts and one passed through gates that connected the different sections.

Beneath the ruler there were three classes or estates: nobles, merchants, and common folk. In contrast with neighboring Sâsânid Iran, which had earlier extended its power here, there was no great gulf between the nobles who lived in castles and the merchant-princes whose homes and estates were equally models of luxury. The Bukharan Kashkath clan was typical of these wealthy and powerful merchants. According to Narshakhî, after the Arab conquerors of Bukhara "solicited" some of their homes, the Kashkath built "seven hundred villas outside the town," each of which had its own garden, park, and servants' quarters.[10] To guard themselves, Sogdian rulers and high nobles had their own *châkar* units, highly trained elite soldiers, whom they supported, educated, and even fictively adopted to ensure their loyalty. They were noted for their bravery. Some of them may be depicted on palace wall paintings in Samarkand. The *châkar* units were recruited mainly from the common folk.[11] Such military retinues were common in the warrior societies across ancient and medieval Europe and Central Asia. Far from the courts of the powerful were the peasants who worked the land. Although mostly technically free, they were often under the power of a *dihqân* (land-owning aristocrat). Because of debt some of the peasants were forced into a status resembling that of the serfs of Medieval Europe.

Sogdia's far-flung contacts created a cosmopolitan, highly sophisticated, and cultured society, one characterized by a commercial, secular outlook.[12] While interested in and tolerant of different religions, Sogdians were also very much caught up in the things of this world. This is evident in the extraordinary wall paintings that have been preserved in the ruins of the Sogdian city of Panjîkand (also spelled, Penjikent, Pendzhikent). It was briefly the capital of Dêwâshtîch, a ruler who titled himself the "King of Sogdia." Many of the homes, including those of the less well-to-do, were decorated with wall paintings and other artwork reflecting a blending of cultures. For example, one wall is decorated with paintings of the tale of the goose that laid the golden eggs, well known to readers of Aesop's fables. Another room has a female orchestra attired in Chinese clothing. Yet others depict tales, with many variants known in India and China, of swindling in business ventures[13]—themes known all too well to Sogdian merchants.

There are statues of Iranian deities such as Anahid, a goddess of fertility, who is shown holding fruit. There are representations of animals following traditions that go back to the Scythian "animal style." There are woodcarvings of figures in flowing attire that appear to be inspired by Indian art There are also works of monumental sculpture, again religious in theme. Wonderful examples of these sculptures could also be found in neighboring Bactria. The most famous of these, perhaps, were the giant statues of the Buddha in Bamiyan, Afghanistan, destroyed by the Taliban in 2001.

All of these urban cultures produced a considerable literature, much but not all of which was religious in content. Some told didactic moral stories. There is a tale much like the biblical story of Job about a man who gains great wealth and has many wives and children on whom he lavishes spectacular wedding feasts. He is much admired by his fellow-townsmen. Then his life falls apart. His children and grandchildren die and he loses everything. He is so reduced in social standing that even the slave-girls are above him. Unfortunately, we do not know how the story ends, as only a fragment has survived.[14] Secular documents include epic tales, love stories, law codes, and government correspondence such as the archives of Dêwâshtîch found on Mt. Mugh. Literacy was fairly widespread. Merchants, of course, needed to keep records of their commerce, routes, and products. Less formal writing has been found in the countryside, where common folk wrote on everyday objects such as clay utensils, as well as on walls.

The mix of cultures is most clearly reflected in religions. In sharp contrast to the medieval Near East and Europe, Sogdia had no state religion and widely practiced toleration. Manichaean, Christian, and Buddhist texts written in Sogdian testify to the breadth of their interests. Buddhism was still widespread in the neighboring former Kushan-Hephthalite territory, co-existing with the worship of many local gods and goddesses, such as the cult of the Amu Darya (Oxus River). Central Asian cities near China, such as Kucha, Qocho, and Khotan, had already been Buddhist for several centuries. These cities were noted for their Buddhist scholarship and translators of Buddhist texts from Sanskrit into Chinese, Khotanese Saka, and Tokharian. One of the early principal translators into Chinese was Kumarajiva, a Tokharian nobleman from Kucha. Chinese Buddhists came here for study.

Xuanzang and later Chinese travelers found only a few remnants of Buddhism in Sogdia proper, where it was probably never strong. He states that the ruler and people of Samarkand were fire worshippers. The city had "two religious foundations" (meaning Buddhist temples), "but no priests dwell in them."[15] The *Tang shu*, however, says that "they honor the Buddhist religion; they make sacrifices to the god of the heavens."[16] The latter was a reference to Mazdaism. Overall, Buddhism fared better in the Sogdian colonies in the East. In addition to pre-Zoroastrian cults focusing on natural elements (fire, water, earth, air), Sogdians and Khwarazmians venerated the mythical Iranian hero, Siyâvûsh, who was associated with birth, death, and rebirth. The people of Bukhara believed that he built their citadel and sacrificed a rooster in his memory annually, before dawn on *Nawrûz*, the Iranian New Year's Day (corresponding to the spring equinox in late March). *Nawrûz* is still widely celebrated in Iran and Central Asia.

Mazdaism had many local variants in Iranian-speaking Central Asia, but without the state-supported priestly hierarchy typical of Zoroastrian Iran. People worshipped a wide array of deities, including individual, family, local, and regional cults. Neighbors often had different favorite gods, which their families considered their special patrons.

A deva in Buddhism was a supernatural being or deity. This deva was found in Tumshuk, a medieval Buddhist center in modern Xinjiang, China. Bildarchiv Preussischer Kulturbesitz / Art Resource, New York

Bukharans also worshipped a Mother Goddess, Anahid (Persian Anahita), Gopatshah, a god with a human head and an ox's body, who was considered the primal force that produced life; and others. The Persian Zoroastrian chief god, the leader of the good, Ahura Mazda, appears in Sogdia as Khurmazta Bagh (the "god Khurmazta"). Sogdian gods also included Zarvana, sometimes called the "king of the gods," Washeghn, or Wishaghn (Persian: *Verethraghna*, god of victory), Nanaiya (a non-Iranian, Mesopotamian or Elamite goddess whose cult had spread among Zoroastrians), Parn ("good fortune," "royal glory") and others known to the larger Iranian world along with Shimnu, the leader of the forces of evil (Ahriman of Zoroastrian Persian tradition). Weijie, a Sui emissary to the "Western Countries," in 610 tells of a Sogdian cult devoted to a celestial deity, whose divine child died in its seventh month. Its devotees, dressed in black, engaged in lamentations every seventh month, while searching the countryside for the divine infant. The Sogdians also venerated their ancestors, making offerings of food and cutting their faces in mourning at the end of the year.[17]

Many Sogdian settlements have the word *vaghn/vaghan* (-*baghn*, -*faghn*, "temple") in their names, indicating that they were clustered around temples. Al-Bîrûnî, the eleventh-century Khwarazmian polymath and author in Arabic of important works on history, geography, philosophy, theology, mathematics, calendrical systems, and astronomy, notes a number of Sogdian and Khwarazmian festivals that were clearly associated with local Zoroastrianism. For example, there was a feast which fell on the fifteenth day of the month of Basâkanaj (the fourth month of the Sogdian year) that allowed people to again eat leavened bread after having abstained, for an unnoted period of time, from eating or drinking anything that had been touched by fire. At a mid-year holiday on the second day of the month of Faghakân, people gathered in the fire temples and ate a special dish made of millet, butter and sugar.[18] Unfortunately, al-Bîrûnî does not explain what role these feasts (many of the names of the holidays contain the word *khwâra*, "eating") played in the religion.

The widespread devotion to idols clearly distinguishes Central Asian Zoroastrianism from its idol-lacking Persian form. The idols, made of wood and clay, were bedecked with jewels and precious stones. Chinese accounts, such as the *Sui shu*, mention a golden idol associated with the spirit "Desi" in the region of Ishtikhan (called "Cao" in Chinese) in Sogdia to which people, sometimes as many as one thousand at a time, made daily sacrifices of five camels, ten horses, and one hundred sheep.[19] The cult of Desi was widespread. The origins and precise functions of these idols within the local religious systems are not always clear. Some may reflect Hindu and Buddhist influences. The idols were so numerous that when the Arabs conquered Samarkand they burned a stacked pile of them that reached as high as a castle.

According to Chinese accounts, on New Year's Day the king and people of Kang (Sogdia) put on new clothes and cut their hair and beards. They held an archery contest on horseback for seven days in a forest near the capital. Whoever hit the target (a gold coin mounted on a sheet of paper) became king for a day.[20] In Ferghana, the contests were less friendly. There, two champions, each representing rival aristocratic factions, fought to the death. This would determine whether it would be a good year or a bad one.[21]

In addition to Buddhism and local cults, there were followers of Nestorian Christianity, which accented the human nature of Christ. They were in the entourage of the Persian Shah Kavad when he fled briefly to Central Asia. Some remained to carry on missionary work. Nestorianism reached China through Central Asia in 635. From their base in Merv, the Nestorians established a center in Samarkand in the early sixth century, successfully proselytizing among Turkic and subsequently Mongol tribes. The Turkic war prisoners whom the Persians sent to Constantinople in the 590s, who had crosses tattooed on their foreheads as talismans against plague, may have been their converts. By the seventh century, Samarkand had a metropolitan. In many respects, after the Muslims, Nestorians became the most successful religious community in this region. Sogdian merchants, as with other religions, also served as missionaries.

The Arabo-Islamic conquests in Central Asia and elsewhere stemmed from a variety of motivations: religious fervor, land hunger, war booty, and a diversion from the growing strife in the Islamic heartlands. Muslims entered *Mâ warâ'nahr*, "that which is beyond the (Oxus) river," the Arabic rendering of Transoxiana, after the death of the last Sasanid monarch, Yazdigard III, felled by a unknown assassin in 651, and Iran's submission to the Arabs. This was part of larger Arab offensives which the Umayyad caliphs (ruling 661–750), the eventual successors of Muhammad (d. 632), and political leaders of the expanding Muslim state, directed against the Khazars, a Türk successor state in the north Caucasus; the western Türks in Transoxiana; and the Berbers of North Africa. Arab armies advanced to Afghanistan and raided across the Oxus, the dividing line between Central Asia and the Middle East, into Sogdia, which had been under loose western Türk rule. China replaced the Türks in 659 as the Arabs began their raids. By the 690s, the western Türks had revived, and a complicated situation developed in which China, Tibet, the Türks, and the Arabs competed for control.

In 705, Qutaiba ibn Muslim, the Umayyad commander in the east, transformed Arab raids into wars of conquest. In the political checkerboard that extended from the Oxus to China, Qutaiba skillfully exploited local Sogdian and Türk rivalries. Some Sogdian merchants in Merv even helped to finance the Arab expeditions. It was good business and they received their share. In quick succession, Qutaiba took Bukhara, Khwarazm, and Tokharistan (in Afghanistan). By 712, he was ready to deal with Samarkand.

Ghûrak, the ruler of Samarkand, was under siege. The Arabs ambushed a special force of Sogdian nobles and warriors sent to relieve the city. They cut off the heads of the slain, wrote their names on their ears, attached them to their belts, and returned, thus bedecked, to Qutaiba. Word of the disaster soon spread and resistance crumbled. Ghûrak, with no hope of succor, surrendered. In the treaty of 712, the Arabs recognized—or perhaps bestowed on him—the title of King of Sogdia. It was in their interest to set up a ruler who was under their thumb. The Arabs, having defeated an eastern Türk army in 713, considered their control over Sogdia and Khwarazm secure.

The Muslim conquerors suffered from their own domestic political disputes. Qutaiba, feeling vulnerable, revolted and perished in 715. Arab hegemony in Transoxiana immediately buckled. The western Türk attempt to reassert their independence from their eastern kinsmen after the death of Qapaghan Qaghan in 716 further complicated the situation. The Sogdians, sensing an opportunity, staged a major revolt against the Arabs in 719. Dêwâshtîch, who also claimed to be king, sided with the rebels.

The Mount Mugh documents give us a brief glimpse into the era. In one letter to Dêwâshtîch "the lord, Sire, the great bulwark, the Sogdian king," written just as the Arabs were reasserting their authority, the writer, "the worthless slave Fatufarn," an agent of Dêwâshtîch, reports that he has brought letters to the rulers of Châch (Tashkent), Ferghana and others as well as information that was too sensitive to be written down, but which he duly reported "orally, fully without omission." From Ustrushâna (another Sogdian statelet), "I did not hear any good news. Even the country of Ustrushâna has been completely evacuated. And my lord, I am alone without a companion and, my lord, I did not venture to go."[22] Rumors were swirling that other lands had reached agreements with the Arabs. Regrettably, only bits and pieces of this dramatic correspondence have survived. The Arabs captured and crucified Dêwâshtîch in 722. Meanwhile, Ghûrak juggled alliances with the Arabs and the Türks. The Arab hold remained uncertain. By 728 it was reduced only to Samarkand and a few other regions. Sogdian rebels found willing allies in the Türks and Tibetans.

As Arab rule faltered, the western Türks revived under Sulu of the Türgesh tribe, who had muscled aside the nominal western Türk qaghan. The Türgesh formed alliances with Tibet and occasionally with the Arabs or with anti-Arab Sogdians as the constantly changing circumstances dictated. Western Türk-Türgesh incursions into Xinjiang worried the Tang, who encouraged divisions among the Türks, pitting Sulu against the qaghan. Tibetans, Türgesh, and Arab rebels joined to threaten Muslim rule beyond the Oxus. The great prize of this clash of empires and their local allies was control of the Transoxanian Silk Road.

In 736–37, the Tang defeated the Türgesh and routed the Tibetans. The Arabs badly mauled Sulu in 737. According to the tenth-century Arab historian al-Tabarî, he was murdered in his sleep shortly thereafter by Bagha Tarqan Kül Chur, a rival, following a dispute over a game of backgammon. The next day, the Türks left Sulu's stripped body, "scattered," and began "making raids on one another."[23] Sulu's demise splintered the Türgesh, ending their challenge to Arab control. Bagha Tarqan Kül Chur ran afoul of China and perished in 744, just as the Uighurs became the new masters of the eastern Türk lands. The Qarluqs, a Turkic tribal union hitherto allied with the Uighurs, broke with their overbearing new rulers the following year, fleeing into the western Türk lands where the Tang were again dominant.

A clash between the Muslims and China, the two remaining empires with interests in Central Asia, was inevitable. A local power struggle in the Sogdian city-states provided the spark, bringing a Tang army and its Qarluq allies to face a Muslim army near the Talas River in Kazakhstan in 751. The defection of the Qarluqs, increasingly rivals of the western Türks-Türgesh, gave the victory to the Muslims. It has long been claimed that Chinese who knew how to make paper were among the captives taken to Samarkand, and from them paper was introduced to the larger Mediterranean world. Recent studies indicate that China had been exporting paper as early as the third century; it was already known in Xinjiang and Sogdia, carried there by merchants and Buddhist pilgrims, before Islam. Central Asia may have been the source for papermaking technology in the Muslim Middle East, but it was not necessarily connected with the events of 751.[24]

The Arab victory, followed by China's withdrawal from Central Asia because of civil wars (755–763), paved the way for Islam to become the dominant religion of Transoxiana. As Muslims strengthened their hold over the Sogdian city-states, some Sogdians fled eastward, joining communities of their kinsmen in the Central Asian-Chinese borderlands.

In the Middle East, the Arabs carried out one of the most successful colonialist enterprises in history. Large numbers of Arabs settled in the conquered territories, including the Transoxanian-Persian borderlands. In the Semitic Middle East, Arabic largely replaced kindred Aramaic, spoken by local Christians and Jews. Islam was initially the religion of a conquest elite. Conversions took place gradually. Muslims did not constitute a majority in Mesopotamia until well into the ninth century. In Syria and Egypt it took even longer. Iran, however, one of the earliest of the conquered lands to achieve a Muslim majority (perhaps by the mid- to late-ninth century), retained its own tongue—Persian—and unique culture.

In Central Asia, over the next few centuries, the bulk of the urban, Iranian-speaking population converted to Islam. As elsewhere, conversion emanated out of the cities where Muslims and non-Muslims interacted most directly. In some areas, the new faith blended with older beliefs. Converts were slow to give up old ways. Conquest provided the groundwork, but conversions, usually voluntary, often had a mix of motives, spiritual, political, social, and economic. The commerce-minded Sogdian and Khwarazmian merchants saw the advantages of being part of the growing Islamic world. The prominence of Persians and Central-Asian Iranians in the newly established ʿAbbâsid caliphate and the improved status of non-Arab Muslims in general in the ninth century were also contributing factors in conversion. Although the caliphs' control weakened in the tenth century, local Islam, now firmly grounded in the cities, reached into the countryside. By the eleventh or twelfth century, it had become largely Muslim as well. The old land-holding gentry, the *dihqân* class, had faded, replaced by a new Muslim elite.

The cities prospered and the government built forts and inns along the caravan routes, promoting long-distance trade. Persian, the "second language" of many people in the Iranian East, gradually supplanted its "kinsmen" Bactrian, Sogdian, and Khwarazmian—although there were still cities in which Sogdian predominated into the eleventh century. Al-Bîrûnî reports that the Arabs, after conquering Khwarazm, burned all the books and killed many of their scholars.[25] Nonetheless, something beyond oral traditions must have survived, for he gives an invaluable account of his native region's local customs, calendars, and religious beliefs. The Khwarazmian language seems to have continued to be spoken, perhaps into the fourteenth century. Persian expanded throughout the eastern Muslim world. Iranians called the Muslims *Tâjîk* or *Tâzîk*. In

Central Asia, *Tâjîk* at first denoted Arab Muslims, but in time came to refer to all Muslims of Transoxiana who had adopted Persian speech.

Central Asia pioneered the development of modern Persian as a literary tongue. It replaced its Aramaic alphabet with the Arabic script and borrowed a considerable number of Arabic words. Persian, however, was not the only language that was assimilating Sogdian-speaking peoples. Turkic, the language of the political overlords of much of Central Asia, had made substantial inroads as well. In the late eleventh century, Mahmûd al-Kâshgharî, a Turkic lexicographer writing in Arabic, could point to cities in which the population was bilingual, speaking both Turkic and Sogdian. Elsewhere, he notes that Turkic dominated in the cities and the local Iranian languages survived only in the surrounding villages.

In Xinjiang, the scene of fierce Chinese-Tibetan struggles in the eighth to early ninth century, the situation was different in many respects. The Arab-Muslim armies had not reached here. Islam gained a foothold only by the later ninth and tenth centuries. Nonetheless, major and long-lasting ethnic and linguistic changes were occurring. The Tanguts (Chinese: Xixia), a people of Tibeto-Burmese affiliation from northwestern China, overran the Gansu Uighurs from 1028 to 1036, other Uighur statelets in Xinjiang preserved their independence in their drive to create their own state over the next two centuries. The Gansu Uighurs survived as an ethnic grouping, the Yellow Uighurs, one of the few remaining Buddhist communities among the Turkic peoples. The Xinjiang Uighurs preserved their independence. They shared a common faith with their Iranian and Tokharian subjects: Buddhism. Uighur Turkic gradually began to replace the local languages, a process largely completed by the time of the Mongol conquests. The Uighurs, having settled and intermarried with their subjects, were themselves transformed, becoming the middlemen of Chinese trade with the western regions. What is today called Xinjiang had indeed become eastern Turkistan.

CHAPTER FIVE

Crescent over the Steppe: Islam and the Turkic Peoples

The migrations touched off by the fall of the Türk Empire and Uighur seizure of power in Mongolia brought Turkic tribes westward to the borders of Irano-Islamic Transoxiana and occasionally into the Black Sea steppes. These tribes, now in direct and sustained contact with the Islamic and Byzantine empires, formed the ethnic building blocks of the Turkic peoples of modern Central Asia.

The Qarluqs came in 745 to the Semirech'e region in southeastern Kazakhstan and in 766 supplanted the western Türks as the leading local power. For a brief time after the Uighur collapse in 840 they claimed leadership of the Turkic nomads, calling their ruler the "Qaghan of Qaghans." The explosive Oghuz appeared in the neighboring Syr Darya region in the 770s, expelling the Pechenegs, another Turkic people, whom they disparagingly called the "Hairy Shaggy Dogs,"[1] ultimately into the Black Sea steppes. Successive Pecheneg migrations, in turn, forced the ancestors of the Hungarians first from Bashkiria into the Black Sea steppes and then, in the late ninth century, into east-central Europe. Central Asian nomadic migrations not only reconfigured the steppe tribes, but also had an impact on Europe's political and ethnic structure.

In the last quarter of the eighth century, the sprawling Kimek qaghanate formed in western Siberia, a mix of Turks, Tatars, and other elements from the Mongol-Manchurian borderlands. The Kimeks effectively exploited the lucrative fur trade with the northern forests and the resultant long-distance trade with the Muslim world. In the first half of the eleventh century, their subjects, the Qïpchaqs, dismantled the Kimek Qaghanate, forming a stateless tribal union from the Danube to western Siberia.

North and east of them were the Kyrgyz, whose ruler still bore the title of Qaghan and resided in a town, Kemijkath, named after the Kem (Yenisei) River. Muslim geographers held them in low regard. remarking that "these people have the nature of wild beasts...are lawless and merciless...[and] are at war and on hostile terms with all the people living round them."[2] Some of their tribes were accused of cannibalism.

Such reports were a mix of fact and fantasy that was typical of accounts of distant peoples. Although remote and living in both the forest and steppe worlds, the Kyrgyz supplied musk, furs, lumber, and ivory to the Silk Road trade.

These states and tribal confederations spoke more or less mutually intelligible dialects of Turkic and followed similar nomadic lifestyles. They were as likely to fight one another as they were to raid the settled lands. The Muslim oasis cities traded with them but also built forts to keep marauding bands at bay and to stage raids into the steppe.

By the early ninth century, the Muslims had developed a brisk trade in slaves coming from the Eurasian northlands and steppe zone. The Khazar Qaghanate (mid-seventh century to between 965 and 969) on the Volga was one of the two main suppliers of slaves. The Sâmânid amîrs (819–1005), a dynasty of governors of Transoxiana, nominally subject to the 'Abbâsids, were the other. They drew on two sources: Turkic nomads captured in warfare and the Slavs of the eastern European forests and agricultural zones, taken in slave raids. The name "Slav" became so closely associated with this dreadful commerce that our word "slave" comes from it.

The Turkic slaves were mainly sold to the 'Abbâsid caliphs who sought human military machines that would follow orders and as aliens would not be subverted by the competing political and ethnic factions in the caliphate. The Turks, non-natives of the Middle East and famed for their martial skills and endurance, were ideal for such a purpose. The Arabs called a military slave *ghulâm* (plural *ghilmân*, literally "boys") or later *mamlûk* ("slave, one who is owned"). Al-Jâhiz, an Arabic essayist of possible Ethiopian descent, who wrote about ethnic questions and the Turks in particular, extolling the Turks' hardiness, said that they spent "many more of their days on the back of a horse than on the ground."[3] Once brought into the caliphate, a *ghulâm* received further training and was inducted into special forces.

Central Asian models, such as the Sogdian *châkar*, may have influenced the shaping of the *ghulâm* institution. In addition, a number of Sogdian and Turkic nobles from Central Asia voluntarily entered caliphal service. Many of the Turks rose to very high military and court posts and in time came to control the caliphate. Indeed, one prominent *ghulâm* of ninth-century Baghdad was Itakh, a Khazar, who began his career as a slave-cook in a wealthy Baghdad home. Ultimately, the military slave institution weakened 'Abbâsid authority as caliphs were made and unmade by the powerful Turkic commanders. This was hardly what the caliphs had hoped for.

The ruling house of the Khazars appears to have been of western Türk Ashina origin. It broke away around 630–650 and formed a state in the North Caucasian, Ukrainian, and south Russian steppes. Prolonged warfare with the Arabian caliphate (between the 640s and 737) for control of the Caucasus ended with a border established in the North Caucasus. The Khazars also defeated the Bulghar union in the Ukrainian steppes, forcing some Bulghars into the Balkans around 679. These Bulghars conquered Slavic tribes that had earlier migrated to what became Bulgaria. In 864, the Balkan Bulghars, who were already assimilating with the Slavs, converted to Christianity, producing the Bulgarian people of today. Elements of Central Asian culture continued nonetheless. For example, a Bulgarian king list (going up to the ninth century) uses a mixed Bulghar Turkic-Slavic tongue and gives the regnal years according to the Twelve-Year Animal Cycle calendar, still widely employed in East Asia and previously widespread among the Turkic peoples.[4]

The Khazar Qaghanate, controlling the Volga route, a major thoroughfare for goods coming from the Baltic and the northern European forests to the Islamic world through the Caspian Sea, became one of the great trading emporia of the medieval world. Khazaria, often—but not always—allied with Byzantium, interacted politically and economically with Constantinople and Baghdad in a complex triangular relationship. A Khazar princess even married a Byzantine ruler. Byzantine emperors rarely married foreign women. Atil, the Khazar capital on the lower Volga, bustled with foreign merchants as well as representatives of the twenty-five subject peoples of the Khazar Qaghans. Muslims (most probably the majority of the resident foreign merchants), Christians, Jews, and pagans were found there. Each group had the right to be judged by the laws of its own religion. The Khazar Qaghan converted to Judaism between the late eighth and early ninth centuries, and many of the Khazar ruling clans followed him. Others remained pagan, continuing the shamanist practices that were typical of the Turkic peoples of that era. Yet others converted to Islam or Christianity. They continued to regard the Qaghan as a nearly divine figure who was a talisman for the good fortune of the state. A sub-Qaghan was entrusted with the day-to-day governance of the realm. The local Muslims included the chief minister of state. He and the personal guard of the holy qaghans were of Khwârazmian descent and had long been resident in Khazaria.

The Sâmânids were even more important in the slave trade. They were Iranians, probably from Tokharistan (in Afghanistan). Descended from local lords who converted to Islam during the Umayyad era, they had achieved local prominence in the early ninth century. Their raids into the Turkic steppe netted some of the early Turkic slave-soldiers. The Sâmânids turned this into a business, even founding schools to train the slaves for service. Expeditions such as that of 893, led by the Sâmânid Ismâ'îl, who called himself "the wall of the district of Bukhara,"[5] brought in some 10,000 to 15,000 captives, including the wife of the Qarluq chieftain.

From their capital in Bukhara, the Sâmânid amîrs became patrons of a brilliant revival of Persian literature. Central Asian scholars from the Sâmânid orbit were major contributors to Islamic and world culture.

The mausoleum in Bukhara was built in the tenth century for the remains of Ismâ'îl ibn Ahmad, whom the 'Abbâsid caliphate rewarded with the governorship of Khurâsân for his suppression of rebels in the east. His power extended into Transoxiana and the Turkic world, where he actively propagated Islam.
Bridgeman-Giraudon / Art Resource, New York

The mathematician Abu Ja'far Muhammad al-Khwârazmî (ca. 780–850), a native of Khwarazm, became one of the astrologers at the court of the caliph al-Ma'mûn. The English word "algorithm" is a distortion of his name. In addition to his contributions to the development of algebra, he wrote on geography and astronomy.

Muhammad al-Farâbî, from the Syr Darya region, became one of the great polymaths of his era. Schooled in Sogdian and Persian, he published his works in Arabic. After teaching in Bukhara, he later settled in Iran and eventually in Baghdad and Damascus. Such mobility was not uncommon among Muslim scholars of his era. His works dealt with a wide range of subjects: philosophy, political theory, ethics, the natural sciences, medicine, mathematics, literature, linguistics, and music. He had much to say about ancient Greek thinkers such as Plato, Aristotle and Euclid. Some of his studies, for example *Fusûl al-Hikam* (The Judgments of Wisdom), were widely used as textbooks in schools of higher learning throughout the Muslim world. His *Kitâb al-Mûsîqî al-Kabîr* (Great Book of Music) dealt with the acoustics and mathematics of music as well as composition. Al-Farâbî's ideas were still influencing European musicologists in the nineteenth century.

Ibn Sina (known as Avicenna in Europe), who came from the area around Bukhara, somewhat overshadowed al-Farâbî. Son of a Sâmânid bureaucrat, a brilliant student in virtually all fields of knowledge, Ibn Sina as a young man gained access to the ruler's library after having cured the Sâmânid *amîr*, Nûh ibn Mansûr. As the Sâmânid regime began to crumble, he left Bukhara and traveled widely, finding shelter with the Khwârazmshâh and ultimately in Iran. He was frequently persecuted for his unorthodox religious beliefs and even accused of atheism, a charge that could bring the death penalty. He earned his living as a medical doctor, sometimes at the courts of various rulers, taught and wrote on everything from medicine (more than 40 books) to cosmography, philosophy (some 185 studies), theology, music, and botany. He, like other scholars of his age, took the Graeco-Roman heritage that had been translated into Arabic, systematized and reworked it, and added his own interpretations. Ibn Sina placed a great emphasis on experiments and acquiring empirical knowledge rather than relying on theory and tradition alone. His *al-Qânûn fi at-Tibb* (Canon of Medicine) was translated into Latin and other languages and widely used in Europe.

The Sâmânid role in spreading Islam was no less significant. Islam, now the dominant faith of urban Central Asia, was expanding into the steppe. The Sâmânids developed *madrasa*s, Islamic colleges, based

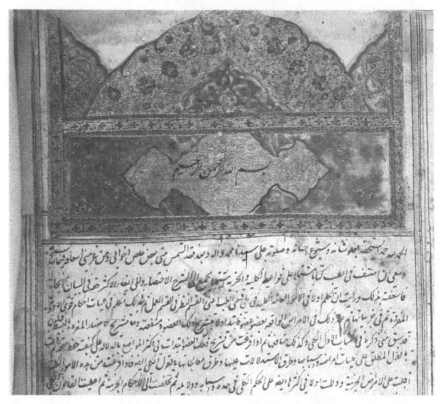

This detail from the manuscript of the Canon of Medicine, *an Arabic encyclopedia, dates to about the fifteenth century. It consists of 492 folios, many of which are illuminated with colored inks and gilding. The great care taken in producing the manuscript is proof of the high value placed on the contents. Gerard of Cremona, who lived in Toledo, Spain, a center for the transfer of Arab learning to the Western world, translated the text into Latin in the twelfth century.* Courtesy of the National Library of Medicine

perhaps on Buddhist models, as well as bureaucratic structures and traditions of governance that Islamized Turkic peoples subsequently brought into the Near East. In theory, the Sâmânid *amîr* was supreme. His chief minister oversaw the government, which consisted of the court and ministries that handled finances, foreign affairs, internal security and other matters. The lines between the ministries and the court were often blurred. Similarly, the power of the *amîr* could vary from time to time and place to place. The Sâmânids were the principal figures of the eastern Islamic world, the heirs of the mercantile traditions of the Sogdian trading cities and major players in transcontinental commerce.

Sâmânid coins (or their imitations) have been found in considerable numbers in Russia and Scandinavia, attesting to the scope of their commercial importance.

Islamic authors portray the Muslim frontiers of Central Asia as an area of unceasing *Jihâd* (war for the faith), and the Sâmânids were anxious to present their conquests as part of the expansion of the *Dâr al-Islâm* (Abode of Islam). Turkic converts also wanted to demonstrate their fervor for their new faith by fighting their pagan kinsmen. Although some of these conquests resulted in the conversion of local lords and their followers to Islam, ultimately it was not the sword alone that brought the religion to the steppe people. Political advantage, along with unnamed missionaries, often merchants and subsequently Muslim mystics called *Sûfîs* who sought an ecstatic spiritual union with God,[6] also played a role. The word *Sûfî* comes from Arabic *sûf* (wool), a reference to the simple woolen garments that the early devotees of this movement wore. In Persian they were called *darvîsh* (poor), rendered in English as dervish. Originally a movement of individuals, Sûfîsm subsequently formed orders or religious brotherhoods. Orthodox Muslims often viewed them with suspicion. Muslim merchants, later followed by mystics, ventured into the steppes, establishing business contacts with nomadic chieftains and patterns of reciprocal hospitality. Commercial and social bonds quietly expanded into a common religious communion.

Some of the Sûfîs, who arrived later, were charismatic, colorful, eccentric people who in many ways resembled Turkic shamans. They often appeared in outlandish attire; some shaved off all body and facial hair and wore only horns and loincloths. Like shamans, it was believed that they could transform themselves into animals, could cure illnesses and had the ability to divine the future. The Turks, already familiar with a variety of religions (Buddhism, Mazdaism, Christianity, Judaism, and Manichaeism), easily accepted this blend of folk Islam and mysticism. Islamic concepts of heaven and hell, for example, were notions for which words already existed in Turkic, although, not surprisingly, they were borrowings from Sogdian. The melding of the Turkic *Tengri* with the Judeo-Christian-Islamic God was not a difficult stretch.

Islam, whether brought by conquest, commerce or mystics, initially came to the Turks from a Persian-speaking world. Muslims were (and still are) divided between the minority Shi'ites, who believe that the caliph should be a descendant of 'Alî, the cousin and son-in-law of the Prophet Muhammad and the father of his only grandsons, and the majority Sunnîs, who believe that the caliphate should not necessarily be limited to the house of 'Alî, but could be given to any worthy member of the Prophet's tribe, the Quraysh. The Islam that came to the steppe was basically Sunnî, but blended, to varying degrees, with local usages that did not fully distinguish it from earlier shamanistic and other practices, such as ancestor worship or the use of dance and chanting to produce ecstatic trances by which shamans entered the spirit world. As with the implantation of any new faith, the implementation of religious orthodoxy took many generations and was often uneven.

The Turkic nomads closest to the Muslim cities of Central Asia first entered the larger Islamic orbit. The Volga Bulghars, unhappy vassals of the Khazars, had close commercial ties with Khwarazm and the Sâmânids. Political and economic considerations moved them towards Islam. Their king converted to Islam, and in 921 requested a delegation from the 'Abbâsid caliphate to build up Islamic institutions in his realm. In 960, according to Ibn al-Athîr, a thirteenth-century Arab historian, "200,000 tents of the Turks converted."[7] The accuracy of the number cannot be verified. Nonetheless, there is no doubt that large groupings of Turkic nomads had embraced Islam. This was probably connected with the conversion of Satuq Bughra Khan, the progenitor of the Qarakhanid dynasty (992–1212), whose state encompassed much of western and eastern Turkestan. When the *khan* or leader converted, his fellow tribesmen usually followed. The tenth century marked a turning point in the Islamization of Turkic western Central Asia. Mass conversions notwithstanding, shamanistic and other elements remained. These included idol worship, one of the worst sins in Muslim belief. Such syncretism is typical of the conversion process. Islamic legal scholars did not regard those who kept the old beliefs alongside the new as real Muslims and considered it legal to take them prisoner in war.

The Qarakhanids, of uncertain origins, ruled over an amalgam of Turkic tribes and crushed the last of the Sâmânids in 1005. As Sunnî Muslims, the Qarakhanids faced no popular resistance when they entered the Sâmânid cities. Ibrahim Tamghach Bughra Khan, the founder of the western Qarakhanid realm, was known for his strict but fair rule and the security he provided. When thieves wrote on the door of the ruler's citadel in Samarkand, "We are like an onion, the more we are cut the bigger we grow," Ibrahim responded under the thieves' graffiti: "I stand here like a gardener; however much you grow I will uproot you."[8]

The Qarakhanid royal house continued Türk political traditions, viewing the state as the collective property of the royal clan and dividing it in two around 1043, each half ruled by a Qaghan and various sub-Qaghans, who awaited their turn on the ladder of succession. The realm was further divided into often poorly defined territorial grants, governed by members of the dynasty and subdivided among vassals. Given the paucity of data, scholars are still debating how the Qarakhanid system worked. The nobility remained nomadic, or seminomadic. Many held an *iqta'*, a revenue grant based on land given in return for state service, somewhat akin to the European fief. The system was, undoubtedly, abused over time and may have contributed to separatist tendencies among the Qarakhanid dynasts and tribal aristocrats.

The economy was essentially unchanged since the Sâmânid period. Archaeologists have found considerable evidence of urban development under Qarakhanid rule, especially in river valleys such as the Talas and Chu, whose inhabitants engaged in agriculture, viticulture, handicraft production, and trade. Some regions had extensive irrigation systems. In the northeastern Taraz area, there was a canal that extended some 100 km (62 miles). The Otrar oasis was crisscrossed with canals, dams, and water delivery systems. Transoxiana and Ferghana continued their ancient traditions of highly developed settled life. There is no evidence that the Qarakhanids attempted to transform farmlands into pasturages.

Nonetheless, their rule adversely affected elements of the old, rural order. The *dihqâns* lost their high social status and the word *dihqân* came to denote an urban artisan or free peasant. In modern Tajik it means "peasant." Subjects paid taxes in the form of produce, labor, or a combination of both. Some peasants fell into debt, lost their lands, and were forced to become sharecroppers. They gave one-third of their harvest in taxes to the government, one-third to the landowner from whom they rented the land, and could keep one third for themselves. Those who were completely bankrupted often sold themselves or family members into slavery. Women, who enjoyed relative physical freedom in nomadic society in the Qarakhanid dominated Irano-Islamic sedentary world, lived largely secluded lives in their homes and could only venture out veiled and accompanied. The sparse information that deals with this era mentions periods of rural or urban unrest.

Another Turko-Islamic state emerged in the later tenth century. In 961, a powerful Sâmânid Turkic slave-general, Alp Tigin, established himself in the city of Ghazni, in southern Afghanistan, which he nominally held for the Sâmânids. One of his successors, Sebük Tigin, made it into an independent state and founded the Ghaznavid dynasty (977–1186). He and his son, Mahmûd, brought much of eastern Iran, Afghanistan, and northern India under their rule while establishing an uneasy border with the Qarakhanids on the Amu Darya. The Ghaznavids raided Hindu India, bringing back enormous wealth and combat elephants. The historian al-'Utbî describes Sebük Tigin's army as having 200 of these elephants, joined together by chains and "all adorned with splendid trappings and incomparable housings." Behind them was a vast army, "assembled, like locusts or ants, innumerable, and as immeasurable as the sand of the desert."[9] The Ghaznavids were the first Muslim forces to use elephants as an essential part of their battle tactics.[10] This military machine was supported by a complex state with Iranian and Indian subject populations ruled by a largely Iranian bureaucracy and a Turkic military elite, the prototype for a number of future regimes.

The Ghaznavids, like the Sâmânids, patronized Persian arts, especially poetry. Many poets flocked to Mahmûd's court. The greatest of them was undoubtedly Firdowsî, the author of the *Shâhnâma*, the Persian national epic poem based on oral and written tales about ancient Iran. Al-Bîrûnî, who came to Ghazni from Khwarazm as the Sâmânids were collapsing, also eventually found support at the Ghaznavid court. He traveled with Mahmûd's plundering armies to India, acquired some Sanskrit, and became one of the foremost experts in the Islamic world on the complex cultures of the Indian subcontinent.

While neighboring states supported and provided a congenial home to the emerging Irano-Muslim culture, the Qarakhanid regime played a seminal role in the birth of Turko-Islamic culture. Under their rule, there appeared original works of literature in Turkic with an Islamic orientation. Following an old genre of "mirror for princes" literature that was popular in the Iranian world and well beyond it, the *Qutadhghu Bilig* (The Wisdom that Brings Heavenly Good Fortune), written in 1069, is a Qarakhanid political treatise set in the form of a dialogue between the ruler and his advisers. They enjoin him to behave with justice, compassion, and equal-handedness to all, great and small. Extolling brainpower and cool-headedness over brawn, they declare: "true nobility belongs to the man of wisdom and intellect."[11]

The author, Yûsuf Khâss Hâjib of Balasaghun, the eastern Qarakhanid capital, cautions that something done in haste out of anger will bring ill, like undercooked food. Punishment should be used only after careful deliberation. The wise ruler "puts his realm in good order so that the common folk become rich, and he in turn makes their wealth a fortress for himself."[12] Yûsuf adds that "a thousand virtues are required for the world-conqueror...With these virtues the world-ruler clears away the fog and grasps the realm; he wields the sword and lops off the neck of his foe; he governs his territory and his people with law and justice."[13] Yûsuf was mindful of the nomadic background of his royal audience. While praising the art of the physician, he (although a Muslim) advises that, along with the medicines doctors prescribe, one should also use the shaman's amulets and incantations.

The brilliant lexicographer Mahmûd al-Kâshgharî produced his *Dîwân Lughât at-Turk* (*Compendium of the Turkic Dialects*, about 1077) in Arabic, a work aimed at the literate Muslim public. He sought to give his audience a fuller understanding of the culture of the Turks, who had now become the dominant military and political force in the Middle East. The *Dîwân* is a treasure trove of data. Many of the lexical entries are illustrated with poems and tales reflecting the Turkic culture of that time. These poems praise the martial valor of the Turks, in particular their victories over their Buddhist and other non-Muslim kinsmen and the defilement of their idols. The vocabulary entries describe all aspects of daily life: clothing, such as an *ichük* (a kind of sable coat) needed for the wintry steppe, furnishings such as *kimishge* (a kind of embroidered felt rug from Kashghar), or occupations such as *bista* (someone who provided overnight lodgings to traveling merchants and guarded their goods).[14]

Qarakhanid rulers could not escape conflict with the *ulama*, Islamic religious authorities, especially in Bukhara. Towards the end of the Qarakhanid era that city had become largely independent and under the control of the Burhân family of Muslim clerics, who held the honorific title of "Pillar of the World." Their opponents, who decried their vast economic and political power, called them "Pillar of Hell." The Qarakhanids, perhaps because of their troubles with the city-based Muslim scholars (who even accused them of heresy) and urban unrest, spent considerable sums on public buildings, ranging from mosques to bathhouses. Archaeological finds indicate that their cities were well kept, by medieval sanitary standards, with places for garbage and sewage disposal in the form of deep pits that were kept covered. The further development of the Silk Road was probably a factor in the urban growth of Qarakhanid cities. While the cities and trade appear to have expanded in the eleventh and twelfth centuries, there is also evidence for the debasement of the silver-based coins issued by the Sâmânids and Qarakhanids in that same period. Historians continue to debate the causes and extent of the "silver crisis."

During the Qarakhanid era, Turkic nomads entered the agricultural regions in larger numbers than ever before. The local population became increasingly Turkic in speech. Turkic served as the language used between linguistically different groups. Anthropologists note, however, that the shift initially was linguistic, not ethnic. The earlier people remained, but now speaking Turkic instead of their earlier languages. The poorer Turks also began to settle. Others, depending on local conditions, became seminomadic, practicing both agriculture and livestock raising.

The conversion to Islam of the Turks had repercussions in the Islamic heartlands. The Seljuks, who became masters of much of the Middle East in the eleventh century, stemmed from Seljük, a war-chieftain of the Qïnïq tribe of the Oghuz confederation. Sometime around 985, he broke with his overlord, settled in Jand on the Syr Darya, and converted to Islam. His sons all had Old Testament names recorded in the sources in their Arabic forms: Mikâ'îl (Michael) Isrâ'îl (Israel), Mûsâ (Moses), and Yûnus (Jonah). This might indicate previous contacts with Judaism or Christianity. In Jand, Seljük and his sons fought against their pagan kinsmen. His descendants joined in the struggles between the Qarakhanids and Ghaznavids, frequently changing sides. There were disturbing rumblings deeper in the steppe. Tribes driven by famine and political turmoil from the Mongol-Manchurian borderlands were advancing westward. Dominoes were falling.

The general turmoil affected Seljük's grandsons, Toghrul and Chaghrï, who fled from the Syr Darya region to Khurâsân (today in eastern Iran and western Afghanistan) by 1034. Hungry and desperate, they raided wherever they could. The disturbances they caused in this revenue-producing Ghaznavid province induced Mahmûd's son and successor, Mas'ûd (ruling 1031–1041), to bring a large army, including Indian war elephants, to secure the area. In May, 1040, Mas'ûd's army, exhausted by the hurried march westward, finally caught up with the Seljuk bands. Toghrul and Chaghrï, joined by other Oghuz bands, unexpectedly defeated what should have been superior forces at Dandânqân. This defeat fatally weakened the Ghaznavids, who now ruled a minor state of the Indo-Afghan borderlands.

By 1042, the Seljuks were masters of an empire that included Khwarazm and eastern and central Iran and were advancing into Transcaucasia. The 'Abbâsids invited them to Baghdad in 1055 to liberate the caliphs from the control of the Shi'ite Buyids. In doing so, the Seljuks became the dominant force in the Sunnî Islamic world. In 1071 Sultan Alp Arslan, Chaghrï's son, defeated the Byzantines at Manzikert in eastern Anatolia and Turkish tribesmen swarmed into much of Byzantine Anatolia, laying the foundations for the Seljuk Sultanate of Rûm ("Rome," that is the eastern Roman/Byzantine Empire) and subsequently the Ottoman Empire Melikshâh, Alp Arslan's son brought the Qarakhanids under Seljuk rule.

Waves of Oghuz Turks streamed into northwestern Iran and eastern Transcaucasia, producing the Azeri Turks of modern Iran and Azerbaijan. Other groups of Oghuz, the Turkmen of today, held northeastern Iran. The Oghuz spread across much of Anatolia, setting into motion a more gradual spread of Islam in its Turkic form into what had been Christian Asia Minor. The adoption of the Turkish language even outpaced conversions to Islam. Some Greek and Armenian populations remained Christian, but adopted Turkish speech. A major ethno-linguistic and demographic shift occurred, reshaping the Middle East. The process produced the modern Turkish people of today. The Turks had not only adopted Islam, but had also become its champions in the Islamic heartlands as well as in Central Asia.

CHAPTER SIX

The Mongol Whirlwind

At the beginning of the thirteenth century, four states reigned uneasily in Central Asia. The Khwârazmshâhs, rulers of a recently cobbled together realm, dominated Transoxiana and parts of the adjoining Middle East. Former Seljuk subjects, they became independent by the latter part of the twelfth century. In 1194, Khwarazmian troops delivered the head of Toghrul III, the last Seljuk ruler in Iraq and Iran, to the Khwârazmshâh Tekish. Tekish's son, Muhammad, master of much of Transoxiana and eastern and central Iran, cast covetous glances at the caliphal throne in Baghdad and at his neighbors, but much of his power was illusory. Khwarazm was an unstable mix of professional Turkic soldiery, restless eastern Qïpchaq tribes with whom the dynasty intermarried, and the settled Irano-Khwarazmian people.

To their east were the fading Qarakhanids, under the aegis of the declining Qara Khitai, also called Qara Qitan, nominal overlords of eastern and western Turkestan. Recent arrivals, they had fled the Jurchen destruction of the Qitan-Liao state in 1124–25. Led by their *Gür Khan* (universal khan), Yelu Dashi, a royal Qitan, the Liao refugees created a new realm in Central Asia. Shamanists, Buddhists, and Nestorian Christians, the Mongolic and Chinese-speaking Qara Khitai imposed themselves on the Turko-Iranian Muslims of Transoxiana. Their religious tolerance, relatively loose system of governance, and the prestige of their Inner Asian and Chinese imperial heritage, made their rule palatable to their Muslim subjects. The Qara Khitai felt no pressure to convert to Islam. Their regime was reasonably successful well into the long reign of Yelu Dashi's grandson, Yelu Zhilugu, but signs of decline became evident by the early thirteenth century.[1]

The Jin dynasty (1115–1234), centered in northern China and Manchuria, arose from the Jurchens, Manchurian hunters and fishermen, who also farmed and raised livestock. Former subjects and now masters of the Liao realm, they dominated the eastern end of the steppe whose inhabitants called the Jin Emperor *Altan Khan* ("Golden Khan," Golden Khan; *jin* in Chinese means "gold"). The Jin had difficulties in controlling the restless tribes of Mongolia. They constantly monitored them, seeking to keep them off balance by promoting internal conflict. The Mongols swept them all away.

The Mongols were one of a number of tribal unions inhabiting Mongolia and adjoining areas in the late twelfth century. Some were steppe nomads, others were hunting and fishing forest folk. Some spanned both worlds. The Mongols, organized in lineages and clans, were centered on the Onan and Kerülen rivers. The historian 'Atâ Malik Juvainî, who came from an eastern Iranian family that previously served the Khwârazmshâhs but had entered Mongol service, describes the Mongols before the rise of Chinggis Khan as lacking a ruler, disunited, and constantly fighting one another. "Some of them regarded robbery and violence, immorality and debauchery as deeds of manliness and excellence." They dressed in the "skins of dogs and mice" which, together with "other dead things" and koumiss, formed their diet. A great man among them was one who had iron stirrups. Such were their "luxuries."[2] The Jin took what they wished from them.

North of the Mongols were the politically fragmented Naiman extending to the Irtysh River in Siberia. Under Uighur influence, Nestorian Christianity had made some headway among them. South of the Mongols were the Tatars, long-time foes—an enmity that the Jin encouraged. The politically ambitious Kereits (in Mongolian Kereyid), led by To'oril, west of the Mongols in the Orkhon and Selenge region, had friendly links with them. Some of them were Nestorian Christians. Less friendly were the Merkit (or Mergid) on the lower Selenge and south of the Baikal region. North and east of them were the Oirats (or Oyirad) and other Mongolic forest folk.

The Tatars, often proxies of the Jin, were politically dominant and their name was frequently used to denote all of these peoples. Mongol unification began with Qaidu, probably in the late eleventh and early twelfth centuries. The *Secret History of the Mongols*, an anonymous Mongol work of the thirteenth century, reports that Qaidu's grandson, Qabul, "ruled over all the Mongols"[3] and was their first khan. When Jin attempts to subordinate him failed, they invited Qabul to a banquet. Fearing poisoned food, he secretly regurgitated everything he ate. The Jin were amazed and then angered when he defiantly tweaked the beard of Altan Khan.[4] Relations worsened when the Jin helped the Tatars to capture Ambaghai Khan, Qabul's successor. He was subjected to a gruesome death, nailed to some kind of torture device, around 1160. Ensuing Mongol struggles with the Tatars were largely unsuccessful, and the Mongols were soon fighting among themselves.

Qara Khitai clothing, especially battle dress, with its Northern Chinese and Manchurian influences, seems to have been distinct from that of their Central Asian neighbors. Qara Khitai weaponry, at least what is known of it, does not appear to differ considerably from the lances, bows and arrows, and iron and leather armor used by their Central Asian contemporaries. This depiction of a Qara Khitai comes from an early seventeenth-century Chinese book of illustrations and may be fanciful. Picture of a "black" Ch'i-tan, preserved in the Ming work, *San-ts'ai T'u-hui*, in Karl A. Wittfogel and Feng Chia-Sheng, *History of Chinese Society, Liao (907–1125),* Transactions of the American Philosophical Society, New Series, vol. 36, 1946, page 625.

This was the strife-torn world in which Chinggis Khan was born sometime in the mid-1160s. Mongol tradition says that he was born "clutching in his right hand a clot of blood the size of a knucklebone,"[5] an omen of things to come. His family claimed descent from the legendary Alan-Qo'a, a widow who miraculously became pregnant when a "resplendent yellow man entered by the light of the smoke-hole or the door top of the tent" in which she slept, rubbed her belly and having entered her womb "crept out on a moonbeam or a ray of sun in the guise of a yellow dog."[6] Qabul Khan was a sixth-generation descendant of Alan Qo'a. His grandson was Yisügei, who named his son Temüjin (blacksmith) in honor of a slain Tatar foe. Temüjin, who became Chinggis Khan, came from a family with a high sociopolitical standing. At the age of nine, he was engaged to Börte, a ten-year-old of the Qonggirad, and left with his future in-laws in keeping with Mongol custom. Yisügei cautioned that his son, who in adulthood would be called "Conqueror of the World," was afraid of dogs and asked that care be taken in that regard.

After Yisügei was fatally poisoned by vengeful Tatars in 1175, his family was abandoned by the other clans. Temüjin returned home. His mother Hö'elün fed her children on "crab apples and bird cherries...wild garlic and...wild onion" and chided them for bickering among themselves, saying "we have no friend but our shadow."[7] The future ruler had an impoverished, but adventure-filled youth, living by his wits—and often as a brigand and horse thief. As a youngster, he and his brother Qasar coolly killed an older half-brother, Bekter, in a dispute arising over captured game.

Temüjin's success as a warlord and adroit politician brought him a following of ambitious young men. These *nökürs* (boon companions), who gave up clan and tribal loyalties, formed the core of his military retinue, providing the future generals and administrators of the Mongol empire. Temüjin's alliance with the Kereit leader, To'oril, his father's former *anda* (sworn blood brother, a very important relationship in Mongolian society), raised his visibility as a young man of promise. An important victory in 1184 by Temüjin, his *anda* Jamuqa, and the Kereits, over the Merkits who had kidnapped his wife Börte, gained him more followers. By 1189, some Mongol factions recognized him as khan. In 1196, allied with the Kereits and the Jin who had turned against their former allies, he defeated his old foes, the Tatars. The Jin, still attempting to stoke rivalries among the Mongolian tribes, honored To'oril with the title *Ong Khan*. In 1202, Temüjin decimated the Tatars, enslaving those whom he permitted to survive. He then destroyed his *anda* Jamuqa and To'oril. Temüjin prized loyalty, but he removed anyone who blocked

This portrait of the great conqueror Chinggis Khan, painted when he was in his sixties, shows him in simple attire. In a letter to a Chinese scholar, he claimed that he wore the clothing of a simple nomadic herdsman, showed concern for his troops as if they were his "brothers," and ate the same food. National Palace Museum, Taipei, Taiwan, Republic of China his path to dominion. In 1206, a *quriltai* (assembly) elected him *Chinggis Khan*, a title that probably meant "universal emperor."

The drive to unify the Mongols and other nomads of the eastern steppes was a reaction to Jin manipulations of local Mongol politics and a growing engagement with the outside world. Chinggis was not the only man in Mongolia with royal ambitions. He was simply better able to capitalize on his foes' divisions. He was also lucky, having several times escaped captivity or the plots of his enemies through a convenient turn of fortune. He not only acknowledged his luck, but advertised it as a sign of divine favor. Like the Türks before him and drawing on the same steppe imperial tradition, Chinggis and his successors would claim the mandate of heaven. Subsequently, Muslims saw him as the "Scourge of God," a notion his propagandists were only too happy to encourage.

The name "Mongol" now spread as a political name to the various peoples of Mongolia that Chinggis had conquered. In the Muslim lands and Europe, however, people would call them "Tatars." Even today, the name "Tatar" lives on as the name of peoples who are overwhelmingly of Turkic origin, but were part of the Mongol Empire. This new realm was centered in the old "holy" grounds of the Türks in Mongolia. The choice was hardly accidental, as this was sacred territory to the nomads, the seat of previous empires. Chinggis and his successors, while employing familiar symbols of power and sovereignty in the steppe, such as possessing "holy" grounds, assuming venerable imperial titles (khan or qaghan), and proclaiming a law code for the realm, also broke with earlier patterns. Chinggis splintered the tribes, knowing how destabilizing they could be to his imperial enterprise, and demanded that loyalty to him replace the bonds of tribe, clan, or family. He reorganized them into the familiar military units of 10, 100, 1000, and 10,000 (the *tümen*), but shorn of tribal affiliations—a standing professional army loyal only to him and his house.

Without the prospect of continuing gain, nomad-warriors would soon abandon a warlord. To retain followers, the successful state-builder had to lead them to further military success—and booty. Chinggis prepared a program of conquest. The Siberian forest and forest-steppe peoples (Kyrgyz, Oirat) and the Önggüt Turks in the Gobi quickly submitted. The Tanguts became tributaries in 1209. In that same year, Barchuq, ruler of the Tarim Basin Uighurs, cast off Qara Khitai overlordship and in 1211 formally swore allegiance to Chinggis Khan, who rewarded him with a royal princess as bride and deemed him his "fifth son." Chinggis made use of the now largely settled Uighurs, effective intermediaries between the steppe and sedentary worlds, who became his bureaucrats. The

Mongols adopted the Uighur alphabet, still used in Inner Mongolia today.

The Mongol assault on the Jin began in 1211, and by 1215 they had taken one of their capital cities, Zhongdu (now Beijing). Jin resistance continued, and operations in Manchuria expanded into Koryo, the Korean kingdom, whose pacification took fifty-eight years. The main focus of Mongol attention, however, was Qara Khitai and Khwarazmian Central Asia. Güchülük, a Naiman prince defeated at the hands of the Mongols in 1208, had taken refuge with the Qara Khitai. Gathering up Naiman and Merkit refugees (also opponents of Chinggis Khan), he exploited the uneasy Khwarazmian-Qara Khitai relationship, posing as ally of one or the other.

Güchülük married Qûnqû, the daughter of the Gür Khan Zhilugu; she was a strong-willed woman who fell madly in love with the Naiman adventurer at first sight. Zhilugu indulged his daughter and permitted their marriage three days later. This would have fatal consequences. Exploiting a Khwarazmian victory over a Qara Khitai army, Güchülük captured Zhilugu and seized control of the state in 1211. He allowed his father-in-law to remain as titular ruler, but he and his Naimans now held effective power.[8] When Zhilugu died in 1213, Güchülük proclaimed himself *Gür Khan*. The local Muslim population, facing demands that they convert to either Christianity or Buddhism favored by Güchülük, grew restive.

The Mongol whirlwind was about to sweep into western Turkestan. While Khwarazm and the Mongols exchanged embassies, covertly seeking information about each other, Chinggis decided to crush Güchülük. He attacked the Merkits again and invaded the Qara Khitai lands from 1216 to 1218. Güchülük perished. Merkit refugees retreated to the Qïpchaq lands, but they and the Naiman no longer presented a military threat.

As the Mongols pressed on the Khwarazmian borders, fears heightened. Muhammad Khwârazmshâh's Qïpchaq kinsman massacred a Mongol trading party. The causes of this senseless provocation, which occurred not long after the Mongol ambassadors had signed a peace treaty, have long baffled historians. A Mongol delegation demanding justice for the victims and compensation for their goods was also put to the sword. The now inevitable war commenced in 1219, and Muhammad's armies simply melted away. He fled and ended his days hiding on an island in the Caspian. Meanwhile, Bukhara and Samarkand, both pillaged, fell in 1220. Thirty thousand craftsmen from the latter were handed out to Chinggis Khan's sons and relatives as booty. A survivor from Bukhara reported that the Mongols "came, they sapped, they burnt, they slew, they plundered and they departed."[9] Central Asia was now under Mongol rule.

Eastern Iran fell next, and the Mongols probed Transcaucasia and the western steppes in force. They defeated the Qïpchaqs, the only remaining nomadic force capable of resistance, along with their allies from Orthodox Christian Rus' (the ancestral core of Russia, Ukraine, and Belarus') in May 1223. On their return east, the Mongols, laden with booty, dealt the Volga Bulghars a glancing blow. The Rus' were stupefied by the suddenness of the attack. Clergymen pronounced it a punishment from God. The Mongols, having familiarized themselves with the region, would return. Chinggis Khan's oldest son, Jochi, was entrusted with this mission.

Chinggis now turned to unfinished business on his immediate borders. His armies subjugated the Tanguts in 1226–27, but in the course of the campaign the aging conqueror fell ill. He died in August 1227. His oldest son, Jochi, had predeceased by several months. Chinggis, although inclined towards his youngest son, Tolui, bypassed him and his second son, Chaghadai, selecting his third son, the amiable Ögödei, as his successor. The *quriltai* of 1229 reaffirmed his choice. Ögödei, although known for his qualities of justice, intelligence, and judgment, was overly fond of drink. Tolui, in keeping with nomadic tradition as youngest son, the *odchigin* (prince of the hearth), received his father's ancestral lands, personal possessions, and the largest allotment of troops, some 101,000. All of his sons concurred.[10]

In principle, the Great Qaghan was the first among equals. Each brother received an *ulus*, literally a "nation, state, people," in essence a state within the larger, still unified *Yeke Mongghol Ulus* (Great Mongol State), and military forces. The initial borders of each *ulus* were not always clearly defined, nor did they together comprise all the conquered territories.[11] Following nomadic tradition, the oldest son received the most distant of his father's holdings. Jochi's sons, led by Batu and Orda, held the western frontier: the Qïpchaq steppe (part of which remained to be conquered), western Siberia, adjoining areas, and anything to the west that the Mongols could take. Batu established his capital, Saray, near modern Astrakhan on the lower Volga. Chaghadai, the abrasive and punctilious keeper of the *Yasa*, the Mongol law code established by Chinggis, initially received much of the former Qara Khitai realm, eventually holding most of eastern and western Turkestan. Ögödei at first had lands in Jungaria (northern Xinjiang), southern Siberia, and territory extending into the Irtysh region. Later, he would have central Mongolia, where he built the imperial capital Qaraqorum in 1235.

The *quriltai*s of 1229 and 1235 charted future conquests. By 1241, the Mongols had subjugated the Qïpchaqs and the Rus' principalities.

The conquest of the Qïpchaq steppe brought large numbers of Turkic nomads under Chinggisid rule. They became a major part of the "Mongol" or "Tatar" forces that swept across Eurasia. The Mongols also gained control of virtually all of the horsepower of Central Asia, which meant almost half of the world's horses.[12] This gave them a tremendous military advantage. Severe climate conditions also contributed to Mongol success. Unusual periods of cold, heavy rains, hail, and strong winds in the 1220s and 1230s in North Asia and extending into Russia, precipitated perhaps by volcanic eruptions, may have played havoc with crops and undermined the local economies.

Mongol invasions in 1241 briefly brought Poland and Hungary under Chinggisid control. A mixed force of some 20,000 Polish and German knights led by Duke Henry the Pious of Silesia was defeated on April 9. The victors collected nine sacks of ears, and Duke Henry's head was paraded atop a spear. The death of Ögödei (probably from alcoholism) and political tension in Qaraqorum cut short consolidation of their westernmost conquests. The Mongols withdrew; Poland and Hungary breathed a collective sigh of relief.

Operations directed at the Middle East had begun in 1230. The Mongols swept across Iran and Transcaucasia. Kirakos Gandzakets'i, an Armenian historian, compared the Mongols to "clouds of locusts...the entire country was filled with corpses of the dead and there were no people to bury them."[13] The Seljuks of Asia Minor succumbed in 1243 at the Battle of Köse Dağ in northeast Turkey. Iran and Asia Minor were now largely under Mongol rule. The Toluids under Möngke, who had replaced the Ögödeids as Great Qaghans in an intra-Chinggisid power struggle, continued the expansion. In 1253, Möngke dispatched his brother Hülegü to the Middle East to complete Chinggisid conquests there. The 'Abbâsid caliphate fell in 1258. In Baghdad some 200,000, according to Hülegü's own estimate, perished. The Mongols, mindful of the old steppe tradition of not allowing royal blood to touch the earth, rolled up the last 'Abbâsid caliph, al-Musta'sim, in a clothing sack and trampled him to death.[14]

A power struggle between his brothers Qubilai and Ariq Böke following Möngke's death halted Hülegü's further advance. He turned eastward with a substantial portion of his army, leaving his remaining forces to move against the Mamlûks, slave-soldiers of largely Qïpchaq origin, who had taken power in Egypt and Syria in 1250. The Mamlûks defeated an invading Mongol force in the Galilee in 1260, marking the end of the Mongol advance in the Near East. Iran, Iraq, and much of Asia Minor were theirs. An uneasy border was established in Syria. Abu

Shâma, an Arab commentator on these events, wryly noted that "to everything there is a pest of its own kind."[15] Only fellow Central Asians, the Mamlûks, could stop the Mongols.

In East Asia, Qubilai, Möngke's brother and successor as Great Qaghan, built a new capital (Chinese: Dadu, Mongol: Daidu, Turkic: Khan Baliq, "Khan's City") modern Beijing, adopted the Chinese dynastic name *Yuan,* and completed the conquest of China by 1279. Qubilai also launched attacks on Japan from Korea, which had been finally subjugated in 1270. These naval expeditions of 1274 and 1281 were destroyed by typhoon storms that the Japanese called *Kamikaze* (divine wind).

Distance and the growth of diverging family and local interests created ever-widening fissures in Mongol unity. Jochi had fourteen sons, Chaghadai eight, Ögödei seven, Tolui ten. The succeeding generations were equally prolific. Each expected his share. Strains within the Chinggisid "golden family" (*altan urugh*) quickly arose. Möngke had purged many Ögödeids and Chaghadaids, accusing them of plotting to seize power. Although the Jochid Batu helped to engineer the transfer of power to Möngke, the Jochid-Toluid alliance fell apart by the early 1260s as the Batuids and Hülegüids fought over Transcaucasia. The Jochids formed an entente with the Mamlûks, most of whom were Qipchaqs from Jochid-ruled lands, against their kinsmen in Iran.

Although the Toluids also fought among themselves, Qubilai's steadfast opponent was an Ögödeid, Qaidu, often presented as the upholder of Mongol traditions. Qaidu sought to reestablish his family's *ulus,* but not the restoration of the Ögödeid Great Qaghanate. He was never a mortal danger to Qubilai. From his base in southern Kazakhstan, Qaidu exploited intra-Chinggisid rivalries, gained control of much of Turkestan in the early 1270s, and in 1281 formed an alliance with the Chaghadaids, which lasted for two decades. He controlled territory from the Oxus River to the Altay Mountains. His state dissolved in internal conflicts after his death and his collaborators, the Chagahaid khans, subsumed it. We know little about Qaidu personally other than that he was very clever and, unlike his kinsmen, abstemious in his personal habits, shunning alcohol (which had killed his father). His beard consisted of nine gray hairs. One of his daughters, Qutulun, was a formidable fighter who accompanied her father on his campaigns. Her father gave her the right to marry a man of her own choosing. Qutulun insisted that only the man who could best her in combat would be her husband. She remained unmarried for a long time, relenting only when gossip hinted at a more intimate relationship with her father.[16]

Throne and territorial struggles rippled across the empire, splintering the realm. Distinct Chinggisid states took shape: the Ulus of Jochi, the Ulus of Chaghadai and the Yuan dynasty in China and the eastern steppes. Hülegü and his heirs, centered in Iran, took the title *ilkhân* (ruler of a subordinate state) indicating a slightly less exalted standing. In reality, the ilkhânate (1356–1335) was an equal *ulus*.

By the late thirteenth century, the Mongol Empire extended from Korea, China, and Manchuria to Ukraine and Russia. Its sphere of influence included the Balkans and the Byzantine Empire. Iran, Iraq, and Transcaucasia formed the southern border zone. Everywhere, they had faced foes that were weak or divided. Cities were destroyed and looted, populations massacred or carried off. When the conquests ended, the Mongols, aided by local and international advisors, began to rebuild. Religions were left in place. Although Mongol religious tolerance has sometimes been exaggerated, the principal obligation of the various clergies was to pray for the health and good fortune of the Khans, who

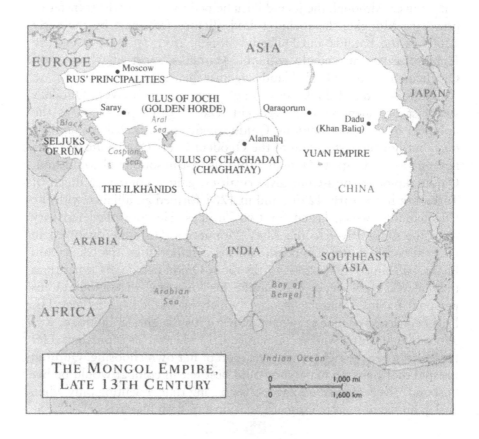

THE MONGOL EMPIRE, LATE 13TH CENTURY

were happy for spiritual support from any source. Moreover, tolerance was also a more realistic policy in a religiously diverse empire.[17]

The Chinggisids were keen talent scouts. Everywhere, their agents identified subjects whose skills could benefit the regime. They, too, were the spoils of war. Linguistic ability in a polyglot empire was especially valuable. Those who knew languages were sure of employment. Qubilai, who spoke colloquial Chinese, was sufficiently concerned with the question that in 1269 he ordered 'P'ags-pa, a Tibetan monk in his service, to devise an alphabet that could render Mongol, Chinese, and other languages of the empire. Despite the ruler's best efforts, it never gained wide acceptance.

The Mongols sought loyal and effective servants in the conquered lands. Chinggis and his heirs were anxious to have specialists who could read (and perhaps control) the heavens. Yelu Chucai, a Sinicized Qitan who served Chinggis and Ögödei, initially gained the favor of the Great Khan through his abilities as an astronomer and meteorologist. Rashîd ad-Dîn tells of a Qanglï Qïpchaq tribesman who was a master of the *yadatash*, the magical rain-stone of the Central Asian Turkic nomads. According to him, this rainmaker was able to produce a snowstorm in summer.[18] Foreign specialists had a pacifying effect on some of the more destructive impulses of the early Chinggisids. It was Yelu Chucai who dissuaded Ögödei from turning much of north China into pasturages for his herds by demonstrating that herding tax-paying peasants could be more profitable.

Skilled individuals moved around the empire as their talents and imperial needs dictated. Bolad Agha, a Mongol, saw service in China and then Iran. There he became one of the most important informants of Rashîd ad-Dîn, the great historian of the Mongol empire. Bolad's father, Jürki, a military commander, was also a *ba'urchi* (cook), or more probably the man who oversaw the preparation of food, in the extended household of Börte, Chinggis Khan's first and senior wife, the mother of his four heirs. This close and intimate contact with the ruling house gave him very high standing. Fluent in Chinese and Mongol, Bolad held many important positions under Qubilai. He also retained his father's title of *ba'urchi* with the aura of easy access to the ruler that it implied. In 1285–86, he was sent to Iran on a mission, and he elected to remain there in service to the Iranian branch of the Toluids. Bolad was probably responsible for introducing paper currency (well known in China) to Iran in 1294. It failed utterly.[19] The production of paper money required printing, which was also brought to Iran, where it met a similar fate.

Rashîd ad-Dîn was a Persian Muslim of Jewish origin who became an important minister under the Ilkhânids. He also began his career in the imperial kitchen, preparing food for the Khan, and personally serving him. This close contact and his natural talents brought him to the fore. His *Jâmi' at-Tavârîkh* (Collection of the Histories) covers not only the Mongols and other Central Asian peoples, but also the history of China, the Near East, and what was known about the West. This kind of broad historical vision would have been impossible without the transcontinental connections established by the Mongols. His overlord, Ghazan Khan, spoke Arabic and Persian in addition to elegant Mongol, and was also acquainted with Hindi, Kashmiri, Tibetan, Chinese, "Frankish," and other languages.[20]

Chinggisid Iran and China exchanged medical and pharmacological knowledge along with culinary arts. Rashîd ad-Dîn possessed a Chinese cookbook and was knowledgeable about Chinese cuisine, probably with Bolad's help. West Asian foods, such as sherbet and soups with chickpeas, were known at the Yuan court. The *Yinshan zhengyao*, a Yuan dietary compendium dated to 1330, is sprinkled with Persian and Turkic terms.[21] Similar interests are seen in a dictionary compiled in six languages (Arabic, Persian, Turkic, Mongol, Greek, and Armenian) by a mid-fourteenth-century ruler in distant Yemen, an area that was never under Mongol control. Among the entries are terms for "chopsticks" and "Chinese duck."[22] The Mongols contributed to a broader Eurasian culinary palate.

Marco Polo is the most famous European who made his way to the Chinggisid courts—and he was a minor figure. His book about his adventures became a best seller in Europe. There were countless others in the Mongol capitals anxious to secure an audience or offer their talents to the Great Khans. William of Rubruck, a Franciscan friar sent by the Papacy to the court of Möngke in the 1250s, mentions "William of Paris," who built a contraption which had the form of a large silver tree which from various apertures spewed forth "koumiss" and other alcoholic beverages. The sharp-eyed friar also appreciated the many alcoholic concoctions prepared from rice, millet, wheat, and honey, which the Mongols borrowed from the peoples of their empire. However, he looked askance at the organized intoxication that was a part of their great feasts, decrying their competition "with one another in quaffing in a thoroughly distasteful and greedy fashion."[23]

Music accompanied the prodigious tippling required of Chinggisid court etiquette, and Rubruck noted the great variety of musical instruments in the "Tatar" camps. The Yuan court maintained an orchestra whose instruments reflected their world empire. An organ was introduced from western Asia, outfitted with a mechanical peacock, which moved in time with the music. Stringed instruments from the Turkic steppe, such as the qobïz, were found in Chinggisid courts, east and west. Ibn Battûta, the early-fourteenth-century North African Muslim traveler, attended a Mongol feast in China in which performers sang in Persian, Arabic, and Chinese. In Iran there were performances of Chinese music.[24] Archery and wrestling were major forms of popular entertainment. Mongol khans gathered wrestlers from throughout their realm. One famous "Tazik" champion was exempted from his wrestling duties and commanded to sire children—future champions. Various forms of polo-like equestrian sports were extremely popular from China to the Mediterranean. The Mongols, thus, may have been the first promoters of international championship sports competitions.[25]

The Chinggisids and the Mongol elite were active players in the exchange process, making their influence and tastes felt in the lands they governed and beyond. Cultural exchange went through a Mongol filter. For a time, the Mongol Empire created a space in which peaceful, secure cultural interaction could occur. The exchange of information created an awareness of wider horizons among the educated and some intrepid men of commerce, who gained a more accurate sense of the world. Chinggisid rule left a relatively small linguistic footprint. Islamic "Turko-Persia" did not become Mongolian in speech. Mongol settlers adopted local languages. The Mongol tongue remained largely limited to the Mongols themselves.

When the Mongol regimes collapsed and trade was disrupted, western Europeans, on the periphery of this commercial interaction, were anxious to find alternate routes to the East. The Muslim Middle East fared less well. The 'Abbâsid Caliphate, in decline since the ninth century, was swept away along with elements of classical Arabo-Islamic civilization. The domination of the Islamic heartlands by steppe peoples since the arrival of the Seljuk Turks in the eleventh century continued. Islam, as a powerful political-military-religious force, revived under the Ottomans in the fourteenth century. The Ottomans were, at their core, a Turkic grouping on the Chinggisid periphery, one of the many such groupings created by the Mongol whirlwind.

The reverberations of Mongol expansionism were felt in Southeast Asia as well. The Mongol conquest of south China contributed to the movement of Tai populations into the Burmese state of Pagan. From 1283 to 1301, periodic Mongol attacks on Pagan (which was briefly taken in 1287), caused further displacements. There was also Mongol military activity, largely unsuccessful, in what is today Vietnam, Cambodia, and Indonesia. The Javanese kingdom of Majapahit exploited the Mongol presence to establish itself in 1293 and then drove them out. Majapahit subsequently became one of the great suppliers of spices, much in demand in western Europe.

The Mongol Empire marked the greatest incursion of the steppe peoples into settled society. It brought the steppe, the forest zone, and many of the neighboring states (China, Iran, Medieval Rus') into a vast world realm, the largest, contiguous, land empire in human history. It profoundly influenced global history, putting into place international networks of communications, the beginnings of an early "world system"[26] in the period 1250–1350, the precursor of the modern world.

CHAPTER SEVEN

The Later Chinggisids, Temür, and the Timurid Renaissance

In the fragmenting Chinggisid world, Mongols were a privileged minority, one increasingly assimilated by their subjects. As al-'Umarî, an Arab historian from Damascus, noted, the conquered Qïpchaqs mixed with the Mongols and they became "as if they were of one stock."[1] Under Mongol rule, many remaining Iranian-speakers adopted Turkic, a process that had been in progress since the sixth century. Turko-Persian bilingualism continued to be common in cities such as Bukhara and Samarkand. Persian (Tajik) retained its status as a language of high culture and government, but increasingly it had to coexist with Turkic even in the literary domain. Turkic became the politically dominant language of Muslim Central Asia.

The Mongols deliberately shuffled the Turkic nomads about, dispersing tribal fragments to form parts of the Chinggisids' personal armies. When the Chinggisids declined, tribal identities or tribe-like units reemerged, some bearing the names of Chinggisid leaders or other prominent people. This reflected the new emphasis on loyalty to a member of the *altan urugh* rather than the traditional ties of kinship, real or invented.

The change of language and emergence of new identities often preceded or accompanied other forms of cultural assimilation, most notably in religion. Islam radiated out from the cities of Transoxiana to the various Turko-Mongolian peoples, some newly arrived within their orbits. It made its first serious inroads in the Ulus of Jochi, which comprised several distinct "hordes": Great, White, Gray, and Blue. From the sixteenth century onward, Russian sources began to call the now-diminished "Great Horde," the core of the Jochid realm, the "Golden Horde," and this became the name under which it is generally known in later sources. Batu's brother, Berke, was the first Jochid to convert to Islam, probably before he became Khan in 1257. His religious mentor was Sayf ad-Dîn al-Bâkharzî, a Sûfî shaykh from Bukhara. Some Chinggisids and others influenced by him appear to have converted as well. But this did not lead to the proclamation of Islam as the official religion of the Ulus of Jochi. Berke's court still followed many older customs associated with shamanist beliefs. Mamlûk ambassadors to Saray in 1263 were warned not to wash their clothes or even eat snow in keeping with old nomadic water taboos. Water reflected the heavens and Tengri, the celestial supreme god of the pagan Turkic and Mongolic peoples. It could not be sullied.[2]

It is only with Özbek, who converted around 1320, that Islam gained a lasting foothold. The account of his conversion highlights the role of the Sûfîs in converting the steppe peoples. According to this tale, typical of Central Asian conversion narratives, the shamans at his court used their "magical powers" to prepare koumiss and other drinks for him. One day, the presence of Muslim holy men prevented this "miraculous" process from taking place. Özbek decided to hold a debate between the shamans and the Muslims. When neither side emerged victorious, the parties agreed that a more strenuous contest was needed. They heated up two large oven-pits, one for a shaman, one for a Sûfî, and decided that "whoever emerges without being burned, his religion will be true." The Muslims chose Baba Tükles, a very hairy man. He put on body armor and his hair stood up and went through the eyelets of the armor. He then entered the baking oven. His opponent, the shaman, was thrown by his colleagues into the pit and immediately perished in the fire. Baba Tükles, over whose oven-pit a sheep was roasting, continued reciting his prayers. When the fully cooked sheep was removed and the oven door opened, he said "Why did you hurry?" By that time his armor was "glowing red hot," but "by the power of God most high not a hair of the Baba's body was burned." The Khan and his entourage immediately became Muslims.[3]

In the western Jochid steppes, Islam followed the trade routes out of the cities of Volga Bulgharia, Urgench in Khwarazm, and more distantly Bukhara. Nomadic populations further from the cities felt its impact less. Rulers, along with the Sûfîs, promoted the religion, but a shamanistic substratum persisted, sometimes up to the present, in the folk Islam that took root.[4] The recently converted Turko-Mongolian shamanists viewed the wonder-working Sûfîs, much like their traditional shamans who, they believed, could shape-shift and enter the spirit world to effect medical cures. Centuries after conversion, shamans among the Kyrgyz, for example, still performed "cures" of sick people through trances and sacrifices to the spirits. Recitations from the Qur'ân usually followed, showing how the two belief systems had become intertwined. During the severe droughts of 1958 and 1965, desperate Kyrgyz performed animal sacrifices following ancient shamanic traditions—often at the tombs of Muslim holy men![5] Reverence for ancestral animals, such as the wolf, remains widespread in the folk culture of a number of Central Asian peoples. Some Kyrgyz and Uzbek women, although Muslims, still make appeals to Umay, the Old Turkic goddess of fertility, during childbirth.

The adoption of a new religion, however, could not preserve a splintering state. Özbek's sons and grandsons had the unfortunate habit of murdering one another. While there was near anarchy in the ruling house by 1359, Islam increasingly became the religion of the majority of the "Tatars," the now-Turkic-speaking mix of Chinggisid-ruled Mongols and Turkic peoples.

Eventually, Jochids from other branches took over, but domestic peace remained elusive. Tatar instability allowed Dmitrii, the subject prince of Moscow, whose predecessors had mainly distinguished themselves as tax collectors for the Khans, to attempt to assert his autonomy in the mid-1300s. Having defeated a Tatar army led by Mamai near the Don River in 1380, he took the sobriquet "Donskoi" (of the Don) in commemoration of his victory. His failure to appear personally before his new overlord, Toqtamïsh (in Russian, Tokhtamysh), who had seized control of the Great Horde in 1381, provoked an attack on Moscow in 1382. Dmitrii fled and the Tatars looted the city. Nonetheless, Moscow, despite this humiliation, increasingly was able to set its own agenda as Tatar power continued to fragment. It remained a nominal vassal of the Khans until the reign of Ivan III (1462–1505) when the "Tatar yoke" ended.

Toqtamïsh's success was largely due to the assistance he received from Tamerlane, a powerful warlord in the neighboring Chaghadaid realm, an unstable region, beset by frequent succession struggles. Chaghadaid nomads closer to the cities felt the influence of Islam, while those that were further away were anti-Muslim and wary of cities. Despite periodic persecution, Islam was becoming the religion of the Chaghadaid ruling elite by the end of the first half of the fourteenth century, but the tribesmen remained overwhelmingly pagan.

By the mid-fourteenth century, the Chaghadaid realm had split in two. The western part, corresponding approximately to Transoxiana, an old Muslim center, became known as the Ulus of Chaghatay (the Turkic form of Chaghadai). The eastern zone, comprising modern southeastern Kazakhstan, Kyrgyzstan, and Xinjiang came to be called Moghulistan, "the land of the Mongols." Ethnographically speaking, this is inaccurate. The bulk of its inhabitants were Turks and Turkicized Mongols. Muslim authors used the term "Moghul" to denote nomads who were, like the original Mongols, less touched by Islamic civilization. The westerners disparagingly referred to their eastern kinsmen as *Jete* (bandit, wanderer, vagabond).

The Ulus of Chaghatay was a crazy quilt of intersecting alliances and enmities of various tribal entities and the personal armies of the Chinggisid princes. It was here that Temür, better known in Europe as Tamerlane, came to power. His name, transcribed in Arabic and Persian as Tîmûr, means "iron" in Turkic. It is a common name, still widely used in the Turkic world. "Tamerlane" derives from the Persian Tîmûr-i Lang, "Timur the Lame." He walked with a limp in his right leg, the result of a wound, and was missing two fingers on his right hand chopped off by a foe when he was rustling sheep in one of his youthful adventures.[6] He was born some 100 km (62 miles) south of Samarkand into a clan of the Barlas, a Turkicized tribe of Mongol descent.

According to Don Ruiz Gonzales de Clavijo, a Castillian ambassador who visited with him not long before his death, Temür's father, Taraghay, was "a man of good family, allied by blood to the clan of Chaghatay, but he was a noble of small estate, having only some three or four riders to his back."[7] The traditional accounts, recorded by Clavijo and others, present the stereotypical picture of a steppe empire builder, not unlike Chinggis Khan: leadership at a relatively young age, military success, and good fortune. Clavijo recounts that, as a youth, Temür and "four or five companions" regularly stole livestock from their neighbors and, being "a man of heart and very hospitable," Temür shared these with his friends and others at feasts. In time, his reputation as a generous-minded bandit grew and others joined him, eventually numbering "some three hundred." Clavijo comments that he robbed anyone "who came his way" and redistributed his ill-gotten gains to his followers. "Thus, he beset all the highways taking toll of the merchants he came upon."[8]

Temür brilliantly manipulated the deadly tribal and clan rivalries of the Ulus of Chaghatay and by 1370 had become the leading political figure. As only Chinggisids could be khans, Temür never assumed that title. Instead, he enthroned puppet Chinggisids while he actually ruled, legitimating his power by marrying Chinggisid brides. He contented himself with the title *Küregen* (Mongol: *kürgen,* son-in-law). For Muslim audiences, he was simply the Great Amîr.

Temür's primary need was to maintain an effective army despite the instability of his powerbase in the Ulus of Chaghatay. His followers remained loyal to him as long as he kept them active. This meant constant war and plunder, which explains the ferocious energy he brought to his campaigns. Fortunately for him, his opponents were weak and divided. He justified his wars by presenting himself as acting in the name of the Chaghadaids or Ögödeids or as the champion of the *Pâdishâh-i Islâm* (the Emperor of Islam). His real ambition was to restore the united empire of Chinggis Khan—with himself at its head. He was a complex figure. A brilliant military commander and politician, he was also capable of extraordinary savagery. Devastation and slaughter awaited those who did not surrender promptly.

A man of the steppe, the last of the trans-Eurasian great nomadic conquerors, Temür was no stranger to settled society. However conspicuous his professed adherence to nomadic traditions and the Chinggisid mystique, he was also a Muslim, a product of frontier Islam. Although a self-proclaimed champion of Islam, his coreligionists were high on the list of his victims. While he criticized others for becoming overly fond of cities, Samarkand was a major beneficiary of his conquests. The city grew and he named some of the new, outlying districts after cities he had subjugated.

Clavijo describes Samarkand as densely populated, surrounded by orchards and vineyards, which, like the gardens within and outside the city, were irrigated by "many water conduits."[9] Temür built a citadel in which he placed the government offices, the mint, a prison, and two palaces, the Kök Saray (Blue Palace, so called from its blue tiles) and the Bustan Saray. The Kök Saray, according to later accounts, still told today, contained the Kök Tash (blue stone) on which the ruler, perched atop a white rug, was invested with his authority.[10] The palace subsequently became infamous as the site of murderous throne struggles. Temür supported the maintenance and construction of new irrigation canals, something that would have been very alien to Chinggis. Samarkand was the showpiece of his empire, a "trophy" as one recent visitor has termed it,[11] which he dressed up to display the booty taken in his wars. Despite the sumptuous buildings, Temür preferred to sleep in a tent in one of the many gardens and parks in the city. Kesh and Urgench in Khwarazm, which he had badly pillaged as well as other cities, also benefited from new construction. Central Asia was again a great center of international commerce between east and west.

A man of contradictions, Temür liked to have learned Muslims in his entourage, but followed both the Sharî'ah (Muslim holy law) and the traditional steppe law (*töre* or *yasa*). He supported Muslim institutions while his armies enslaved Muslims (which was forbidden by

Islamic law) and destroyed mosques. His soldiers left pyramids of skulls in their wake. Like many of his contemporaries among the nomad elite, he had one foot in the urban Islamic world and the other in the pagan steppe. Many of his followers were still shamanists. Although he campaigned in the steppe for strategic purposes, aside from his core Chaghatay forces he did not try to bring the nomads into his state. Nomads did not willingly become part of powerful centralized states. Keeping them off balance and divided sufficed for his purposes.

To some degree this was a government on horseback. Temür created little in the way of governmental infrastructure. His empire grafted itself onto the already existing bureaucratic and tax-collecting agencies. In time, Temür replaced local rulers with members of his family and others whom he deemed trustworthy. The latter were few.

Temür's campaigns extended from India to Asia Minor, a kind of plundering "tourism" of his neighbors. These were raids for booty, not permanent conquest. Local rulers either submitted and paid ransoms or were subjected to devastating attacks. He defeated his former protégé, Toqtamïsh, repeatedly, even seizing and sacking Saray. The Great Horde never recovered.

While "visiting" Damascus, he conducted a series of "interviews" in 1401 with Ibn Khaldûn, the North African historian and philosopher-sociologist. Temür, although illiterate, knew of the scholar, an indication of the breadth of his interests. Ibn Khaldûn came before the conqueror and kissed his outstretched hand. Temür, who was fluent in Persian in addition to his native Turkic, spoke no Arabic and used an interpreter from Khwarazm. He peppered the scholar with questions about North Africa and asked him to write a description of the region for him. Ibn Khaldûn, who spent more than a month in the conqueror's camp, produced the requested book (which does not seem to have ever been published). He was impressed with Temür's intelligence, knowledge, and curiosity. A consummate diplomat, the great historian flattered his host, telling him he was the greatest conqueror in human history—and did not neglect to give him gifts, an essential part of "Tatar" court etiquette.[12]

Temür's less pacific side, however, was amply on display in 1402, when he defeated and captured the Ottoman Sultan Bâyezîd at the Battle of Ankara. The Ottoman ruler died shortly thereafter in captivity and the Ottoman push to take Constantinople was set back for half a century. Returning to his capital, Samarkand, in 1404, Temür held audiences with Clavijo and somewhat dismissively with representatives of the Ming dynasty, the newly established ruling house of China. This was to be his

During a siege, nomads found and exploited weaknesses in a city's defense system—and then poured in. Cities that resisted were looted and their populations terrorized, typical of warfare in much of Eurasia. The attack on Bhatnir, to which many refugees had fled, was a preface to Tamerlane's sacking of Delhi in 1398.
Bildarchiv Preussischer Kulturbesitz / Art Resource, New York

next target. The aged conqueror set out for the east but died of natural causes the next year.

In contrast to the dynasty's founder, his descendants were literate. They patronized scholars, poets, architects, and artists. Some historians argue that the Timurids, with their emphasis on promoting culture and meritocracy, were like the Renaissance monarchies of Europe in which cultural displays became essential parts of governance. Shâhrukh, Temür's son and successor, based in Herat (now in Afghanistan), and his wife, Gawhar Shâd, promoted the decorative arts, such as manuscript illumination and architecture. She built a mosque, *madrasa* (Muslim school of higher learning), and other pious endowments. Gawhar Shâd was also an active force in politics, which proved her undoing. She was killed in a family power struggle in 1457 at the age of eighty.

A passion for the arts and the murder of family rivals became all-too-familiar themes of the Timurid world. Shâhrukh's son, Ulugh Beg, his viceroy for Transoxiana and successor in 1447, was interested in science and built an astronomical observatory that still stands in Samarkand. It was part of a *madrasa* that emphasized astronomy and mathematics. The culture that Ulugh Beg and his circle fostered was bilingual, using both Persian and eastern Turkic. The latter language, developing in the Chaghadaid Ulus, is known as "Chaghatay." Neither Shâhrukh nor Ulugh Beg were gifted military commanders. By 1447, the state was fragmenting, torn apart by grasping relatives, restless underlings, and rebellious vassals. Ulugh Beg, driven from power by his own son, 'Abd al-Latîf, was murdered. Despite the deadly rivalries, Sultan Husayn Bayqara, the most successful of the later Timurids, held forth at a glittering court of poets and artists in Herat. The products of this Timurid cultural flowering resonated across the Turko-Iranian literary and artistic world with admirers in the Ottoman and Mamlûk capitals as well as in India. In Herat, the poet Mîr 'Alî Shîr Navâ'î, the sultan's close friend, composed verse in both Persian and Chaghatay Turkic. In his *Muhâkamat ul-Lughâtayn* (The Judgment of the Two Languages, 1499), he argued for the equal standing of Turkic with Persian. Nonetheless, Persian cultural traditions, even if expressed in Chaghatay, tended to prevail.

Unique among the artists of this era was the still mysterious "Muhammad of the Black Pen" (Siyâh Qalam), who may have been connected with Herat. His richly colored and expressive paintings of everyday nomad life, phantasmagorical demons, and wandering Sûfîs provide extraordinary snapshots of Turkic nomads on the periphery of the Iranian sedentary world.[13] The extraordinary miniaturist Kamâl al-Dîn Bihzâd, a protégé of Navâ'î in Herat, produced an array of portraits

Built in just five years at the start of the fifteenth century, the Bibi Khanum mosque in Samarkand was intended to be the most magnificent mosque of its era. According to one legend, Temür had it built in honor of the mother of his principal wife, popularly called Bibi Khanum (Madam First Lady). Other accounts say Bibi Khanum herself had it built hurriedly as her husband was returning from his looting of Delhi. The hasty construction caused bricks to occasionally fall off, striking believers below. Yet another legend reports that the architect would only hurry the work if Bibi Khanum allowed him to kiss her. She did and Temür had her killed because of it. This photograph shows the mosque in the late nineteenth century. Library of Congress, LC-P87-8052B

(including those of Navâ'î and Sultan Husayn Bayqara) and scenes from the court and the daily life of ordinary people.

The Sûfîs, as individuals and as groups, had played a pivotal role in the Islamization of the Central Asian nomads. Now organized in *tarîqa*s (brotherhoods), they were important factors in Timurid politics, society, economy and culture, some acquiring great wealth. The most influential of these *tarîqa*s was the Naqshbandiyya order founded by Khwâja Bahâ ad-Dîn Naqshband, a Tajik of the Bukhara region. He continued a long tradition in which each Sûfî spiritual leader (called *shaykh* in Arabic or *pîr* in Persian) bequeathed his position and, to some extent, his charisma, to a successor. Unlike the Christian monastic orders to which they bear some superficial resemblances, the Sûfîs were not cloistered. They moved in the world and their hospices were open to it. Many Muslims, in the cities and villages, participated in their rites without becoming fulltime members of the order. The powerful Naqshbandî, Khwâja 'Ubaydâllah Ahrâr, became an advisor to Timurid sultans. His surviving letters are an interesting mix of pieties and concrete "supplications" to assist their bearers. The Khwâja's word carried great weight.

Like the Chinggisids in China, the Timurids developed an effective system of tax collection and other forms of more centralized rule, which alienated the nomads. They retreated to the steppes, reformed, and returned in large, powerful confederations—ultimately to the detriment of the Timurids. In Europe, a new interest in sea power developed as a way around the turbulence of Timurid Central Asia and the increased costs of goods coming via Mamlûk Egypt from the Indian Ocean trade, the hub of much international commerce at that time. The Mamlûk sultan, Barsbay, desperate for revenue, began to heavily tax this transit trade. The Europeans, seeking to bypass this expensive middleman, developed more efficient sea power to gain entry into the Indian Ocean. Ultimately, the shift to maritime routes following Vasco Da Gama's voyage to India in 1498, affected the economy of Central Asia. The land routes had become too dangerous and costly.

The Timurid era witnessed the greater integration of the Turks into Transoxiana and the further Turkicization of the non-Turkic population, demographic trends that were already in motion. Some of the Turkic tribesmen began to sedentarize, perhaps under pressure from their Timurid masters. Settled subjects were easier to control. These two processes, the taking up of a settled lifestyle and the use of Turkic speech, put into place some of the major ethnic and linguistic components of the modern Uzbek people.

Jochid fragmentation equaled that of the Timurids. In 1399, Edigei, previously a general of Toqtamïsh, defeated the latter and his ally, Vytautas (Witold) of Lithuania. Thereafter, he dominated the Golden Horde using various Jochid puppets until 1410. He actively promoted Islam among the nomads in the Qïpchaq steppe—often by force—and proclaimed his descent from Abu Bakr, the first caliph. What was novel here was the attempt to link a respected Islamic lineage with the exercise of political power in the steppe. It did not succeed. In 1419, he perished in an endless swirl of warfare, his body hacked to pieces as an object lesson to non-Chinggisid upstarts. Despite this inglorious end, Edigei's exploits lived on in legend, becoming part of the oral folk culture of the Tatars, Bashkirs, Qara Qalpaqs, Uzbeks, and the Noghais. The latter people, a Turkicized Mongol tribe, were his core followers. They regrouped and in the fifteenth century, now known as the Noghai Horde, became the throne makers and throne breakers in the politically fragmented Chinggisid lands between western Siberia and the Volga.

Throne struggles, drought, and plague in the 1420s exacerbated the ongoing disintegration of the Jochid Ulus. It is a murky period, and the surviving historical records are contradictory. Between 1443 and 1466 (even, perhaps, as late as 1502), three new Jochid khanates took shape in the Crimea, at Kazan on the Middle Volga, and at Astrakhan on the lower Volga. A fourth state, the Kasimov khanate, was created on the Oka River with Muscovite aid in 1452. Any Chinggisid descendent had the right to claim to one or another of these khanates. The Noghais, whose military support was critical, were only too happy to profit from the ongoing political turmoil. The Jochid realm had devolved into a series of unstable states.

Jochid rule over the Volga-Ural region also had ethnic and religious ramifications. The Volga Bulghars blended with the Qïpchaqs and "Tatars" to form the modern Volga Tatar people. Other Bulgharic groupings remained apart from this process, mixed with local Finnic peoples, and did not convert to Islam. They became the ancestors of the modern Chuvash people, some two million today, living next to the Volga Tatars. They are the only people who have preserved the Bulgharo-Turkic language. Notions of a "Bulghar" legacy continue to play a role in defining Chuvash and Volga Tatar identities. Among the Tatars, the Bulghar legacy was associated with Islam.[14] The neighboring Bashkirs of the Ural region also became Islamic but, in sharp contrast to the over-whelmingly settled and relatively highly urbanized Kazan Tatars with whom they have close linguistic affinities, remained nomadic.

East of the Volga-Ural zone, in the forest-steppe zone of western Siberia, the Jochid khanate of Sibir, the northernmost Muslim state, arose under obscure circumstances. Led by Ibaq Khan, a descendant of Jochi's son, Shiban, it emerged as coherent political-military force, often closely associated with the Noghais and hence important in the scramble of Jochid princes seeking to rule the Volga khanates. In 1481, Ibaq Khan and the Noghais pummeled Ahmad, khan of the Golden Horde.

Severely weakened and then buffeted by assaults from the Crimean khanate, the Golden Horde blinked out of existence in 1502.

While the Golden Horde crumbled, new confederations emerged. With Noghai support, the Shibanid Abu'l-Khayr Khan became the dominant force in the western Siberian-Qïpchaq steppes by 1451. His followers, a mix of Qïpchaqs and Turkicized Mongol tribes, called themselves Özbeks, taking the name of the Jochid khan who had converted to Islam. These Özbeks are better known in English by the Russian pronunciation of their name: Uzbek. Abu'l-Khayr Khan's successful raids into Timurid Transoxiana heightened his authority. His "state" extended from the Ural and Syr Darya Rivers to Lake Balkhash and the Irtysh River. He was a harsh man and his drive for dominion produced challenges from other Jochids and subject tribes, but his undoing came from another quarter: the Oirats, a powerful western Mongolian tribal union.

The Oirats emerged from the forest margins of the Mongolic world. Their leaders were politically powerful shamans holding the title *beki*, who early on had formed important marital ties with the Chinggisids. After the collapse of the Yuan dynasty in 1368, most of the Mongols of China returned to Mongolia, where they comprised two large geographical groupings, eastern and western. Organized in *tümen*s, they remained under the control of Chinggisid Great Khans, whose authority waxed and waned in the ever-changing chessboard of Mongol politics. Various khans, including some non-Chinggisids, competed for power. The Oirats, a core element of the western tribes, which sometimes controlled much of Mongolia, eventually became dominant in western Mongolia, Xinjiang, and parts of Siberia to the Irtysh River. The Ming dynasty, hoping to control their turbulent Mongolian borderlands, incited Oirat-Eastern Mongol rivalries.

Under Toghon and his son Esen, Oirat power grew in the mid-fifteenth century. They dominated Mongolia, extending their authority into the Ulus of Chaghatay and eastward toward Manchuria and China, and even captured the Ming Emperor in 1449, whom they held prisoner for a year. As a non-Chinggisid, Esen usually placed a puppet Chinggisid at the helm, but in 1453, he proclaimed himself Great Khan. His own commanders were uneasy with this development, and a personal enemy killed him in 1455.

To the west, only Abu'l-Khayr Khan had the potential to counter the Oirats. The two armies moved toward one another in 1446. Esen's forces greatly outnumbered Abu'l-Khayr Khan's troops. Nonetheless, Esen offered peace, his envoy telling the haughty Uzbek khan, "let not sweat drip from the shirts nor blood come from the bodies of our young men."[15] Abu'l-Khayr Khan refused the offer. He was defeated and took refuge in the city of Sïghnaq in the Syr Darya region. This Oirat encounter was a foretaste of things to come. In 1457, Amasanji, Esen's successor, subjected Abu'l-Khayr Khan to a terrible drubbing.

Other Jochids, Janïbeg and Girey, long chafing under Abu'l-Khayr Khan's harsh rule, now challenged his authority. These "rebels" called themselves Özbek-Qazaq (Uzbek-Kazakhs) and subsequently simply Qazaq, a term denoting "free, independent man, freebooter, adventurer," often with the sense of "rebel."[16] From 1459 to the late 1460s, the Uzbek-Kazakhs, by the thousands, fled Abu'l-Khayr and took refuge in Semirech'e, the region between Lake Balkhash and the Tianshan Mountains, in southeastern Kazakhstan. After Abu'l-Khayr Khan's death, as Mirza Haidar Dughlat records in his history, the Ta'rîkh-i Rashîdî, completed in 1546, the Uzbek state "fell into confusion, and constant strife arose among them."[17] The Uzbek-Kazakhs, today's Kazakhs, continued to grow. By 1466 they already constituted an imposing confederation and were soon prepared to move against the Uzbeks. The modern Uzbek and Kazakh peoples are the products, in part, of what now became a permanent division.

The situation in Moghulistan was chaotic, the result of ongoing Chaghadaid feuding and attempts by the khans to force Islam on often unwilling nomads. The Ta'rîkh-i Rashîdî reports that under the Chaghadaid Muhammad Khan, "if...a Moghul did not wear a turban, a horseshoe nail was driven into his head." The same source reports that a recalcitrant chief converted only after a frail Tajik holy man knocked out his pagan champion.[18] By the late fifteenth century, Moghulistan was becoming Muslim. The Kyrgyz, however, remained largely shamanists or adherents of some mix of Islam and shamanism. Amidst these religious strains, the Oirats constantly threatened the whole of the old Chaghadaid realm. Uwais Khan of Moghulistan fought sixty-one battles with them; he was successful only in one. Nonetheless, he held the region more or less together. After his death in 1428, there was further political splintering.

Changes were also occurring in Xinjiang. In the late fourteenth century, Turfan was still largely non-Muslim. By the sixteenth century, the name "Uighuristân," long associated with Turkic Buddhist and Christian cultures, had faded from memory. The region was fully Islamic by the late sixteenth-early seventeenth century.

The Chinggisid aura by this time was much diminished. The Qubilaid Batu Möngke, known by his title Dayan Khan, reunited the eastern Mongols, after 1483. Orphaned at the age of one, he ascended the throne at seven, marrying the formidable and politically powerful Mandukhai

Qatun (termed his "step-mother" in one local chronicle), widow of Mandagul, a khan of the Chakhar Mongols who enjoyed a certain preeminence. Chakhars are today dominant in Inner Mongolia. The political initiatives probably came from Mandukhai Qatun and her camp.

Mongol chronicles subsequently portray Dayan Khan as the true heir of Chinggis and Mandukhai Qatun as the mother of the nation. He organized the Mongols into six groupings, subdivided into left and right wings. The system, with some variations, continued into the twentieth century.[19] In addition to the Chakhar, the left wing included the Khalkha, who comprise the majority of the population of the Republic of Mongolia (Outer Mongolia). Despite Dayan Khan's successes, internecine strife always lurked under the surface, reemerging after his death. Unity remained elusive. Meanwhile, new empires were forming in the realms bordering on Central Asia, new confederations were taking shape in the steppe, and new technologies were coming to the fore.

In the early tenth century, the Chinese had developed a gunpowder-filled tube, which was attached to a "fire lance," an early flame-thrower. Other devices capable of spewing forth nasty bits and pieces that could tear human flesh were added. By the dawn of the Mongol era, primitive gunpowder weapons were available. The Mongols, ever alert to new military technologies, made these devices known across Eurasia. By 1300, the tubes became larger, barreled, and could now fire a missile. Temür's arsenal included primitive flame-throwers and rockets. It seems very likely that he introduced handguns and cannons to Central Asia, having brought back artillery specialists taken in his Ottoman campaign. The Gunpowder Age had come to Central Asia and Temür contributed to the further dissemination of these new tools of war.

Nonetheless, the nomads, overall, were slow to adopt these new weapons. Their reliability and accuracy, in this early stage, rarely equaled that of the trained archer. Initially, cannons were not very effective against rapidly moving horsemen. Ming guns proved ineffective against Esen Khan's Oirats. It has been argued that the inability of gunpowder weapons to deal effectively with the Mongol threat retarded the development of Chinese weaponry, as the Ming came to doubt their efficacy. Such, however, was not the case in Europe.[20] In time, infantry armed with increasingly accurate gunpowder weapons would prove to be superior to mounted archers. By the late fifteenth century, nomads were no longer able to take the now heavily fortified cities defended by gunpowder weapons. The technology of warfare was moving in a direction that was not favorable to the millennia-old advantages of the mobile, mounted bowman.

CHAPTER EIGHT

The Age of Gunpowder and the Crush of Empires

In the early sixteenth century, Central Asians found themselves increasingly wedged between competing empires on their borders. The Safavid Shâh, Ismâ'îl, heir to a militant Sûfî movement among the Turkish tribes of western Iran and Anatolia, conquered Iran and made Shi'ite Islam its state religion. Shi'ite Iran obstructed Sunnî Central Asia's direct contact with the Ottoman Empire, the most powerful Sunnî Muslim state. In the 1550s, Muscovy conquered the Volga Jochids, erecting further barriers between the Central Asian and Middle Eastern Muslim Turkic peoples. The Mongol adoption of Tibetan Lamaistic Buddhism, in which a supreme religious teacher, the *Dalai Lama*, provided spiritual (and often political) leadership, separated Buddhist Mongols from Muslim Turko-Persia, further splintering the Chinggisid realms. The rise and expansion of the Manchu empire in the seventeenth and eighteenth centuries compounded these fissures.

The balance of military power was shifting—to the detriment of the nomads. In the mid-1600s, there may still have been parity between the nomad's composite bow and the matchlock musket. A century later, the flintlock rifle was becoming the superior weapon. Some nomads rejected the new technology as not suited to their traditional modes of warfare. Others were willing to use it, but largely lacked the industrial capacity to produce the new weapons or the money to buy them. Overall, they fell behind in the arms race. The heyday of the nomad-warrior had passed.[1]

The Kazakh break with Abu'l-Khayr Khan was a catalyst for the restructuring of the Turkic Chinggisid world. Around 1470, the Kazakh tribes, led by Janïbeg and Girey, settled in what is today Kazakhstan, coalescing into a powerful union. *Qazaq*, originally a sociopolitical term, became an ethnic designation. Qâsim Khan, a son of Janïbeg, considered the most powerful ruler since Jochi, controlled much of the Qïpchaq steppe with more than a million warriors.[2]

Pressured by his Kazakh foes, Muhammad Shîbânî (Abu'l-Khayr Khan's grandson) and his Uzbeks crossed into Transoxiana in 1500, driving out the remaining Timurid regimes. One of Shîbânî Khan's

The Mongolian steppe is dotted with lamaseries, the monastic centers of Lamaistic Buddhism. In Mongolia they amassed considerable wealth through the contributions of the faithful, as did monastic orders in Christian Europe, and as a consequence played an important role in politics and the shaping of Mongol culture. Photo by Arthur Gillette © UNESCO

principal foes was Babur, the Timurid prince, poet, and warrior who subsequently took refuge in India. In his memoirs, the *Baburnâma*, Babur paints an unflattering portrait of his Uzbek nemesis. He calls him "Wormwood Khan" and says that he was an illiterate who composed "insipid poetry" and "did and said a multitude of stupid, imbecilic, audacious, and heathenish things."[3] Wormwood was used to make hallucinogenic drugs, hence Babur's contemptuous nickname for him (a play on the similar-sounding Mongol *shibagh*, "wormwood") implied that he was drug-addled as well.

In reality, Shîbânî Khan was well educated by the standards of his time, and his poetry and prose works earned him respect in the demanding literary circles of the region. He was no more given to intoxicants than Babur, who was hardly chaste in such matters. Moreover, Shîbânî Khan was a Muslim in good standing, having become closely allied with the Yasawiyya Sûfîs, who played a significant role, alongside the Naqshbandiyya, in promoting Islam among the nomads. Countering Shah Ismâ'îl's ideological claims, Shîbânî Khan styled himself the "Imam of the Age, the Caliph of the Merciful One."

The Uzbeks transformed Transoxiana into "Uzbekistan." They constituted the military and political elite, but only a minority of the population. They settled among the earlier layers of Turks and Iranians in a complex quilt of languages and cultures. It was the heavily Persianized Chaghatay Turkic, long associated with urbane, Turko-Persian, Timurid civilization, not the Qïpchaq of the new conquerors, that represented Turkic in official and literary circles. The intellectual elite remained bilingual in Persian and Turkic. The culture zone of Turko-Persia stretched from India to the Ottoman Empire. Sunnî-Shi'ite hostility made cultural interaction more difficult, but the Turko-Persian symbiosis continued.

Muhammad Shîbânî Khan was an ally of the Ottomans, his fellow Sunnî Muslims, against the Safavid Shi'ites in Iran. The inevitable war ended disastrously for Shîbânî Khan, who perished in a 1510 battle near Merv. The Safavids sent the skin of his head, filled with straw, to the Ottoman Sultan, a glaring challenge. Some Timurids, with Safavid aid, briefly returned to Transoxiana—only to lose it again to the resurgent Uzbeks in 1512.

Babur was among the Timurids who fled in 1512, first to Kabul in Afghanistan and then to India. He defeated the Lodi Sultans of Delhi and established India's Mughal dynasty (1526–1858). Babur and his immediate successors viewed India as a temporary refuge until they could regain Transoxiana, but their attempts to do so failed. Nonetheless, the Mughals remained culturally oriented towards their earlier homeland. Mughal rulers were still educated in Chaghatay Turkic until the early eighteenth century. As in Central Asia, Persian served as a language of government and high culture. Although Mughals and Uzbeks remained rivals, Mughal India continued to draw on the military, bureaucratic, and intellectual talent of Central Asia. It was a good place for ambitious, talented men to earn well. Some Central Asians remained; others came briefly, complained of the climate and food, made their fortunes, and departed.

The life story of Babur's cousin, Mirzâ Haidar Dughlat, illustrates the troubled nature of the times. When Uzbeks killed his father in Herat in 1508, Babur took him in. His protégé had "a deft hand" in Persian and Turkî poetry, painting, calligraphy, and arrow making.[4] His Ta'rîkh-i Rashîdî is filled with astute observations about events and the people who shaped them. In the service of another cousin, Sa'îd Khan, the ruler of the Yarkand khanate in Moghulistan, Dughlat distinguished himself as a military man and politician, highlighting the multiple talents of the Central Asian elite of that era. In 1541 he took Kashmir and founded his own, semiautonomous statelet. Harsh experience had taught him to seize opportunities when they arose.

To the west, Muscovy was increasingly a factor in shaping the borders of Central Asia from the sixteenth century onwards. The grand princes of Moscow, legitimated by the Orthodox Church and service to the Mongols, brought the other Rus' principalities under their control. After Constantinople fell to the Ottoman Turks in 1453, the Muscovite state saw itself as the last outpost of Orthodox Christianity. Expanding into the Finno-Ugric lands to their east, the Muscovites were soon contesting control over the fur-trapping northern peoples with the Kazan and Sibir khanates. This was the prelude to the Russian conquest of the Volga Tatar khanates, expansion into Siberia, and later into the Kazakh steppes.

In 1552, Ivan IV "the Terrible" of Moscow conquered the Khanate of Kazan. Its population—Muslim Bulgharo-Tatars, Bashkir tribes in the Ural region, and Volga Finnic peoples—all became Russian subjects. Ivan IV took the Khanate of Astrakhan in 1556. The Volga-Ural zone, which had for centuries been under the control of Turkic peoples, was coming under Russian rule. Muscovy was approaching Central Asia.

Having conquered the Volga khanates, Ivan IV, self-proclaimed *tsar* (emperor) since 1547, presented himself as heir of the Byzantine emperors and the Chinggisid khans, a potent ideological claim. Muscovite propagandists depicted his conquests as a crusade against Islam and called for the mass conversion of the Muslim Tatars to Christianity. Churches replaced destroyed mosques, and Islamic proselytizing was prohibited. Thereafter, Moscow's policies, depending on conditions, alternated between Christian missionary activity (sometimes coercive) and toleration. Pagan peoples, such as the Volga Finnic populations, were converted to Orthodox Christianity, often only superficially. Extensive colonization followed. By the seventeenth century, Russians became the majority in these regions.

Tatar nobles, encouraged to enter Muscovite service, quickly assimilated, becoming Orthodox Christians and constituting an important element of the imperial Russian aristocracy. Those that did not, often became merchants or 'ulamâ, the Muslim equivalent of clergy. Subsequently, Volga Tatar merchants and clergy played an important role in the ongoing implementation of Islam among the Turkic-speaking nomads in the steppes.

From 1500 to 1900, Russia, one of the most rapidly expanding states in the world, acquired approximately 50 square miles a day. In its early phase, Muscovite frontier forts were staging points for further expansion and protection from nomad slave-raids. The latter took a huge human toll. Even as late as the first half of the eighteenth century, large numbers of Russians (perhaps as many as 200,000) were being carried off into captivity. This made the Russian lands second only to Africa as a source of slaves.[5]

In 1581, Ivan IV began the conquest of Siberia when a Cossack adventurer and bandit, Yermak Timofeevich, with a force of 840 men, defeated the Khan of Sibir, Küchüm, and sacked his capital, Isker. Yermak died in a Tatar ambush in 1585, but the Russians continued to pound Küchüm. He lost his family (he allegedly had one hundred wives), wealth, and realm and perished sometime after a final defeat in 1598, killed by the Noghais with whom he sought refuge.[6]

Smallpox (popularly termed 'the "Red Witch" in some parts of Siberia[7]) and other diseases decimated the indigenous populations, aiding the Russian advance. Moscow's armies marched across Siberia to the Pacific, erecting strategically located forts as they went. The Russians reached the Pacific in 1638 and founded Okhotsk in the 1640s. Russian colonists followed. The Kyrgyz of the Yenisei River, alternately subjects or rivals of the Oirats for dominion over other Siberian peoples, ended up paying tribute to both the Russians and the Oirats. Russian movement forward halted only when it encountered the Manchu Qing Empire.

The Manchu empire stemmed from the Jurchen peoples of Manchuria, who had previously produced the Jin (golden) dynasty. Although not steppe nomads, they were influenced by Central Asian political traditions. Nurhaci, a Jurchen chieftain, united many of the Jurchens. In 1616, he proclaimed himself khan, taking the name *Aisin* (golden) as his clan name (*Aisin Gioro*, "Golden Clan," was reminiscent of Jin and Chinggisid usages). His son and successor, Hong Taiji, subjugated the eastern Mongols and some northern Chinese.[8] In 1635, he forbade the use of the name *Jurchen* and formally adopted the invented name *Manchu* as the designation of his people.[9] His followers were a complex mix of Jurchens, Mongols and Chinese, many of them bicultural. The next year, he declared himself emperor and took the Chinese dynastic name Qing, which sounded like Jin.

After defeating the Ming in 1644 and firmly establishing their rule in China, the Manchus advanced into Mongolia, Siberia, and the borderlands of Muslim Central Asia. The Russians were approaching the region from Siberia and the western steppes. The two empires met in Siberia. Russia sought trade with China; the Qing sought political stability in their northern borderlands. The Treaty of Nerchinsk (1689) took up the question of borders.[10] Curiously, both sides decided that the official negotiating language would be Latin, which several of the Russian negotiators knew, and in which the Jesuits accompanying the Manchu delegation were fluent. Jesuit missionaries and diplomats had been active in China since the sixteenth century. Both sides used Mongol for unauthorized communications. The 1727 Treaty of Kiakhta stabilized the Russo-Qing boundaries and established Kiakhta, on the Selenge River, as the border trading city of the two empires.[11]

The Russian empire had enveloped the borderlands of Muslim Central Asia from the north and west. The steppe nomads, their remaining obstacle, were politically divided. Competing Mongol factions increasingly sought Moscow's aid against their domestic rivals and China, providing Russia an entryway into Central Asian affairs.

Mongol divisions had multiplied. Unity was ephemeral, rising and falling with charismatic leaders. Buddhism would provide elements of cohesion. The Chinggisid Altan Khan, one of Dayan's numerous grandsons, had again revived the eastern Mongols and warred against China, Tibet, and the Oirats, causing the latter to harry Muslim Turkic Central Asia. Altan's attacks reached the suburbs of Beijing and worried the Ming, who undertook further fortifications, producing the Great Wall of China in the form in which it is known today.[12] The peace that Altan Khan finally established with China in 1571 elevated his stature, assuring him a grudging predominance among his Chinggisid rivals. Altan Khan's lower rank among his grandfather's numerous descendants, and inter-Chinggisid rivalries, had prevented his formal recognition as supreme khan. He took another route: Buddhism.

Tibetan Buddhism had adherents among the Mongols of China. When the Yuan fell, Mongol Buddhism also faded. Tibet, now again under its own monarchy, underwent a religious revival. The *Gelupga* (yellow hat) sect, founded by the reformer Tsongkhapa, promoted the notion of rule by a supreme Lama, a living embodiment of the Buddha. Tibetan missionaries proselytized among the Mongols.

Altan Khan's "sudden" interest in Buddhism began in 1571 with the arrival of the charismatic lama Ashing. Altan dispatched a letter written in gold, inviting a Gelugpa leader, Sonam Gyatso, to Mongolia, declaring that the lama's "unshakable benevolence" should be extended to the Mongols.[13] At their meeting in 1578, Altan Khan bestowed on Sonam Gyatso the title *Dalai Lama* from Mongol *dalai* (ocean, sea), denoting the lama as either an "ocean of wisdom" or a "universal" teacher, and declared him to be the reincarnation of Tsongkhapa, who had died in 1419, and the third in the line of Dalai Lamas.[14] Comparing the lama and qaghan to be "like the sun and the moon," Altan further announced that "in a previous reincarnation," the lama had been 'P'ags-pa and he had been Qubilai.[15] With this one stroke, Altan Khan strengthened the Gelugpa lamas in Tibet and gave his own regime an enduring source of legitimacy—underscoring through religion his connection to Qubilai Khan. In Mongolia, Chinggisid-based rule and Buddhism were now joined. Kökeqota ("Blue City," today's Huhhot, capital of Inner Mongolia), a city he founded as a symbol of his regal status, became an important Buddhist cultural center.

The other major Chinggisid princes quickly converted. Subsequently, visiting Tibetan monks determined that the fourth Dalai Lama was a great-grandson of Altan Khan, known in Tibetan as Yonten Gyatso. An incarnation of the Buddha, the first *Jebtsundamba Khutughtu* ("holy saint," a title given to the highest clergy) also appeared in Mongolia in the form of a Khalkha prince, Zanabazar. He became a major figure in shaping Mongol lamaistic Buddhism, founding a lamasery in 1648. It became the foundations of the city of Urga, today Ulan Bator, the capital of the Mongolian Republic. Succeeding *Jebtsundamba Khutughtu*s, as the spiritual leaders of the Mongols, enjoyed enormous political and economic power. The Oirat conversion came slightly later, around 1620, through the efforts of a Gelugpa-educated Oirat lama, Zaya Pandita, who also reformed the Oirat alphabet and translated 177 Tibetan works into Mongol. At the behest of the Dalai Lama, he traveled tirelessly between the tribes, seeking to foster Buddhism and intertribal peace.

Mongol Buddhists attempted to root out shamanism, the "Black Faith," and end practices such as human sacrifice. When one of Altan Khan's young sons died, the child's mother wanted to have one hundred children and camel foals sacrificed to accompany the prince into the afterworld. Although such sacrifices for royalty were ancient in the steppe world, Mongol society now felt revulsion and prevented the slaughter. Altan Khan's wife became a symbol of evil. When she died in 1585, the Dalai Lama exorcized her corpse, allegedly transforming it into a lizard, which then perished in flames.[16]

A Mongol Buddhist cultural flowering followed; Mongol scholars translated the Tibetan classics and composed important histories, such as the *Altan Tobchi* (The Golden Summary) and the *Erdeni-yin Tobchi* (Precious Summary) The conversion to Buddhism affected all levels of Mongol society. The khans gained a new source of legitimacy as lamas proclaimed them reincarnations of earlier khans. Commoners kept images of the Buddha in their tents and made offerings when eating or drinking.[17] With the conversion, Mongolia and adjoining regions became part of a Buddhist religious and cultural sphere, very distinct from that

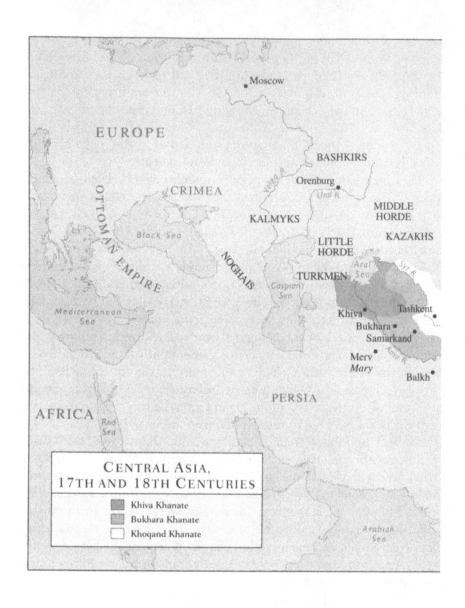

**CENTRAL ASIA,
17TH AND 18TH CENTURIES**

- Khiva Khanate
- Bukhara Khanate
- Khoqand Khanate

of the Central Asian Turko-Persian Islamic lands. Conversion also
assured the dominance of the Gelugpa sect in Tibet and of the institution of the Dalai Lama, as spiritual and political leaders. They, in turn,
trained and influenced many of the Mongol elite and administrators.
After Altan Khan's death, family feuds and the ever-expanding number
of rival khans further decentralized political power. The "one Mongol

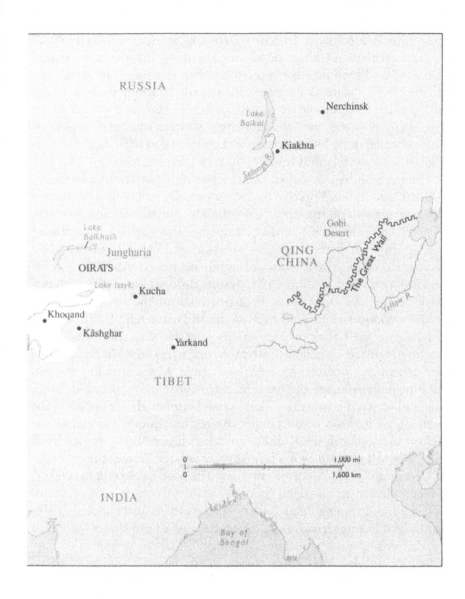

nation" had become many, in reality, paving the way for the Manchu conquest.[18]

By the mid-seventeenth century, Buddhist Mongols hemmed in Muslim Turko-Persia in the east, rival Mughals held the south, hostile Safavid Shi'ites blocked the southwest, and Christian Muscovy loomed in the northwest. The Shibanid Uzbek khanate mirrored the Mongol world in its lack of unity. The early Uzbek khans were relatively effective, but as with their Chinggisid kinsmen in Mongolia, this was a family "business" and each member wanted his own territory. The result was that the Uzbek "state" was more like a confederation. Each Shibanid had the title of *sultan* and an appanage where he was a virtual sovereign. These divisions were the khanate's greatest source of weakness. The khan ruled more by persuasion and cooperation with local notables (officials, clan, or religious leaders) than by law—or force.

The early Shibanids shifted capitals between Samarkand, Bukhara, Tashkent, and Balkh. Effective rulers periodically emerged. The learned poet and patron of the arts, 'Ubaydullâh, Shibanî Khan's nephew, repeatedly defeated the Safavids, restoring Transoxiana to Shibanid control, and beat back a Mughal invasion in 1545–47, all the while checking the acquisitive impulses of family members. 'Abdallâh II, who ruled Bukhara from 1583 to 1598, despite disloyal kinsmen, rebellious Uzbek chiefs, and Oirat raids, brought much of the realm under his authority, conquered territory in Xinjiang and eastern Iran, and reduced the power of the Uzbek military aristocracy. He was solicitous of the economy, regularizing coinage and improving irrigation. His commercial interests included contacts with Ivan the Terrible, who sent an Englishman, Anthony Jenkinson, to Bukhara to learn more about Central Asian trade and to see if a route to China could be secured. This marked the beginning of Russian contact with the region. Immediately after the death of 'Abdallâh II, the Kazakhs invaded, supported by some Uzbek lords. This last attempt of the nomads to conquer Transoxiana failed.

Decentralizing forces came into play. The head of the religious establishment, the Shaykh ul-Islâm, wielded considerable authority, religious, political, and economic. Sûfî leaders such as the Naqshbandî shaykhs, wealthy and exempt from taxes, exercising great power over the khans as their spiritual guides, meddled in politics. As incompetent rulers succeeded one another, the Uzbek commanders, facing growing domestic threats from the Safavids and Kazakhs, opted for a new dynasty led by the brother-in-law of 'Abdallâh II, Jânî Muhammad. Descended from a Jochid from Astrakhan, he had acceptable Chinggisid credentials and marital ties with the ruling house that went back several generations.

The Jânid line (1599–1785), also known as the Toqay Temürids or Ashtarkhânids, began uncertainly and ultimately proved weaker than their predecessors, lacking authority among the Uzbek tribes, the military commanders, and nobles who had become powerful feudal lords. The alliance between the Sûfîs and the dynasty became stronger, with the dervishes emerging as the dominant partner. The Jânids never recovered from a 1740 invasion by Nâdir Shâh of Iran, who had sacked Mughal Delhi the previous year. The last Jânid rulers were largely puppets of their *ataliqs* (chief ministers) from the Uzbek Manghït tribe. These Manghït *ataliqs*, who had been the actual rulers for some time, began to call themselves *amîrs* in 1753. The Manghït Shâh Murâd, son-in-law of the Khan, ended the charade in 1785 and became ruler in his own right. As a non-Chinggisid, however, he remained *Amîr* rather than Khan and hence assiduously courted the support of the religious establishment to gain legitimacy.

By the late eighteenth century, the Uzbek state had split into three separate realms, each ruled by dynasties stemming from local Uzbek tribes whose chieftains had become chief ministers under fading Chinggisids and then taken power on their own. Aside from the Manghïts in Bukhara, the Qungrats ruled in the khanate of Khiva, capital of the old Khwarazmian lands since the seventeenth century, which had achieved full independence from Bukhara in the early eighteenth century. In 1804, the Qunghrat Eltüzer assumed the title of khan. In the Ferghana valley, the chief ministers of the Uzbek Ming tribe effectively became the rulers in Khoqand (Qoqan), a city they founded in the early eighteenth century. 'Âlim took the title of khan, establishing the Khanate of Khoqand (1798–1876). All were beholden to local military chieftains and powerful Sûfî leaders whose formal approval legitimated their rule.

Cultural stagnation accompanied political fragmentation. Once a great center of Islamic learning, Central Asian *'ulamâ* became increasingly caught up in a rigid legalism, which was not unique to this part of the Muslim world. Innovation was a term of upprobrium. Any break with tradition was deemed an assault on basic religious values. Uzbek Central Asia remained on the margins of the rapidly developing and increasingly European-dominated modern world. While Europe had embarked on overseas empire building and experienced the Age of Reason and the Enlightenment, Uzbek Central Asia faced a "brain drain": men of talent were lured to service in Mughal India by high salaries.

The opening of new maritime routes to the East and to the Americas by the Europeans in the sixteenth century and the global crises of the seventeenth century including climate changes (the Little Ice Age), famines, economic depression, population decline, and unending political turmoil, altered patterns of global commerce. Scholars have long viewed these changes as contributing causes of Central Asia's economic marginalization and intellectual stagnation. Recent scholarship has begun to challenge aspects of this view.

Central Asia remained a part of the world trading system, but commodities and routes changed. The flow was more north-south than east-west. Central Asia became a major Russian link to China—although in the late seventeenth century Moscow began to explore more northerly routes as well, cutting off some Central Asian middlemen. Indian merchants formed a network that connected India, China, Iran, Afghanistan, and Central Asia. Caravans to India could be as large as 40,000 load-bearing animals. The ultimate destinations may have been less distant. There was less emphasis on luxury goods, although silks and spices were still carried along these venerable highways. The slave trade flourished. The horse trade, known since antiquity, remained significant. Mughal India, under Emperor Aurangzîb, annually imported 100,000 horses from Bukhara and Afghanistan. Bukhara also exported cattle and fruit (especially melons and grapes) to South Asia. Religious hostility did not prevent commerce with Shi'ite Iran or Christian Muscovy. Bukharan traders brought both local products, ranging from raw silk to livestock, and goods from Siberia (furs), China, and India. Central Asia continued to function as a highway of commerce.[19]

Nonetheless, there were economic realignments producing decline and population loss in some areas. The nomads largely remained behind and disadvantaged in the gunpowder age. They were ill prepared to meet the challenges of rapid technological advances and a mindset that welcomed innovation. Similar problems were apparent throughout the larger Turko-Muslim world. The Ottoman, Iranian, and Mughal Empires, having also undergone the transformation from conquest dynasties to bureaucratic states, were grappling with the challenge of an aggressive Europe and a changing economic and politico-military landscape. European outposts and colonies now dotted Asia and the Americas. For Central Asia, the immediate threats came from Russia and Qing China.

The Kazakhs lay directly on the path of the Russian advance. Political fragmentation, common to other Chinggisid polities, also beset Kazakh society. Unlike the Uzbeks, the Kazakhs remained in the steppe, unable to secure significant urban bases. The khans attempted to impose stricter authority over their subjects, who deposed or sidelined overly harsh rulers. Religion, a potentially unifying factor, was less significant. The Kazakh khans had close ties with the Sûfî orders, which were trying to strengthen Islam among the nomads—often with little more than superficial success. Aleksei I. Levshin, a Russian traveler and ethnographer who journeyed to the Kazakhs in the 1820s, reported that most Kazakhs responded "we don't know" when asked "what is your religion?"[20] Some modern scholars now question the accuracy of Levshin's statement. Many Kazakhs mixed Islam and shamanism, as they had for centuries.[21]

According to popular tradition, by the time of Haqq Nazar Khan (who was assassinated in 1580), the Kazakhs had divided into three groupings: the Great Horde in Semirech'e, the Middle Horde in Central Kazakhstan and southwestern Siberia, and the Little Horde in western Kazakhstan. These names referred to their respective order of seniority. The Kazakhs, despite setbacks, periodically extended their power to the Kyrgyz, Noghais (also torn by internal divisions), and the Bashkirs. By the early seventeenth century, the Kazakhs found themselves surrounded by enemies, especially the Oirats.

The fractious Oirats also faced pressure from all sides. The efforts of Khara Khula to unite them caused one group, the Torghuts, to break away. In the 1620s, led by their khan, Khô Örlökh, some 200,000 to 250,000 Torghuts migrated from the Jungarian basin towards the Ural River and then into the trans-Volga-Caspian steppes, plundering Russian, Kazakh, and Noghai lands as they went. Other Oirats, unhappy with the developing political order in the east, joined him. These western Oirats are better known as the Kalmyks. Although Khô Örlökh died in warfare in the North Caucasus, his sons, Shikür-Daiching and Puntsog, despite violent rivalries with kinsmen and pressures by other Oirats in the east, pushed forward, eventually establishing themselves in the lower Volga region in the 1650s. This marked the founding of the Kalmyk state, a Buddhist power on the Volga.

Moscow sought to use the Buddhist Kalmyks against the Muslim Crimean Tatars and Noghais, who menaced the Russian frontiers. In 1655 the Kalmyks swore an oath of allegiance to the Tsar, but each side understood the agreement differently. The Russians viewed the Kalmyks as "subjects" who would bear arms for the Tsar when called; the Kalmyks considered themselves "allies." By the 1660s, Moscow had become the dominant partner. More Oirat groups from the east joined Ayuki Khan, who, backed by Russia, became the paramount Kalmyk ruler. Moscow provided gunpowder weapons, making his army a highly effective pro-Russian force in dealing with the Crimean Tatars (and more distantly with the latter's Ottoman overlords) and other steppe foes.

In the east, the Oirat Jungars (from Mongolian *jüünghar*, "left wing" of the army[22]) founded an empire. Jungaria, the area of Xinjiang north of the Tianshan, which they occupied, takes its modern name from them. The Jungar chief, Baatur Khungtaiji, continued the program of political unification begun by his father Khara Khula. A 1635 treaty with Russia broadened trading opportunities and enhanced his stature. He received the title of *Erdeni Baatur Khungtaiji* from the fifth Dalai Lama, which elevated Jungar prestige.

Baatur Khungtaiji participated in the 1640 Mongol-Oirat *quriltai* (assembly) summoned to ameliorate inter-Mongol hostilities. It produced the Mongol-Oirat Code, which strengthened khanal authority and established Buddhism as the pan-Mongol religion, perhaps with the hope that this would unify the fractious Mongols. The code granted lamas a privileged status and fined people who invited shamans into their homes. One of every ten men in a family would become a monk. Indeed, Baatur Khungtaiji sent one of his nine sons, Galdan, to Tibet for study. The code also regulated many aspects of private life, encouraging population growth. Young women were expected to marry at the age of fifteen or shortly thereafter, and the sons of four out of every ten households had to marry every year. In keeping with older practices, one could take the wife of an enemy slain in combat.[23]

Galdan, who returned in 1670 from his studies in Tibet, had the strong backing of the Dalai Lama, who gave him the title *Boshughtu Khan* (Khan by Decree of Heaven), providing ideological support for his imperial ambitions. As non-Chinggisids, the Jungarian rulers had been hesitant to use the title *khan*. This title legitimized Galdan's royal status, recognized in both Russian and Qing correspondence with him. At home, however, his nephew, Tsewang Rabtan (who later ruled as *Khungtaiji*), whose bride-to-be he had stolen, frequently challenged him. Nonetheless, Galdan, now possessing cannons (the technology coming from Russia), which he transported on camels, made his Jungars one of the great powers of Central Asia, bringing Tibet and Xinjiang (1677–1678) under his sway and menacing the Khalkhas in the east.

The three empires, Russian, Qing and Jungar, anxiously probed one another. A Qing general reported that Galdan was "violent and evil, and addicted to wine and sex,"[24] but hoped to have him maintain order among the Mongols not yet under Manchu rule. In return, they would give him trading rights, which always enhanced a leader's standing in the steppe world. The Russians also offered him trading rights, repeatedly stressing that he should serve the Tsar, but fended off his attempts to bring them into anti-Qing coalitions.

The Jungars built up an urban center at Kulja on the Ili River, brought in east Turkestani peasants (subsequently known as *Taranchi*, "farmer") to grow food and attracted European and Chinese technicians. Galdan's establishment of a settled base, a system of tax collection, coinage, and a weapons industry (producing gunpowder, armor, and hand weapons) showed that his was not an ephemeral steppe structure, but a state with imperial ambitions.[25] His spy network of lamas worked to win over Mongols under Qing rule.

Giuseppe Castiglione, an Italian Jesuit who served at the court of Qianlong, was a gifted painter and architect who depicted scenes from Qing life. Here he captures the movement of cannons borne on the backs of camels, along with advancing infantry forces. This movable field artillery allowed Galdan, the Jungar ruler, to continue to exploit the time-honored mobile style of warfare favored by the nomads. Library of Congress, LC USZ-62-44377

Galdan's expansionism troubled his neighbors. Many of his Mongol rivals, who had not already done so, joined the Manchus, as did the Muslims of Xinjiang. In 1690, the Qing emperor, Kangxi (ruling 1661–1722), ordered his commanders to "pursue and destroy him [Galdan] without mercy."[26] In 1696, a massive Qing army of 400,000 delivered a crushing blow. Galdan, near starvation and losing followers daily, died the next year, perhaps of natural causes—or from poisoning. He was cremated. The Qing, to dishonor him, reported him a suicide. They captured one of his sons and publicly executed him. After some haggling, Tsewang Rabtan, surrendered his uncle's head and ashes to the Qing, who ceremonially destroyed them in Beijing in 1698—a message to opponents of Manchu rule.

The Jungar threat remained under Tsewang Rabtan, the only independent Mongol ruler in the Qing borderlands. His imperial ambitions drove his neighbors into Russian or Qing arms. Jungar depredations against Tibet in 1717–18 inclined the Gelugpa towards the Qing. In 1720 Tibet joined the Manchu orbit. Following Kangxi's death, Tsewang Rabtan unleashed devastating raids against the Kazakhs, who found themselves caught between the Kalmyks and the Jungars. Kazakh tradition refers to the period of 1723–26 as the "Great Calamity" (*Aqtaban Shubïrïndï*, literally "the bare-footed forced migration"), a mass flight exacerbated by harsh weather and famine in which as many as two—thirds died. Fleeing Kazakhs descended on the Uzbeks lands; others headed towards the Russian and Kalmyk borders.

In 1731 the khan of the Little Horde, Abu'l-Khayr, seeking a counterpoise to the Kalmyks, accepted Russian protection. The Middle Horde (1740) and Great Horde (1742) soon followed. Viewed as a temporary political maneuver, the relationship brought neither peace nor security. Rather, it marked the beginning of direct Russian control in the Kazakh steppe. The centuries-old struggle of the Kazakhs, Kyrgyz, and other Turkic peoples of Central Asia against the Jungars and Kalmyks is preserved in epic narratives still recited today, such as the *Alpamïsh* tale known to virtually all the Muslim Central Asian Turkic peoples, and the *Manas* tale which is the Kyrgyz national epic.

In 1757 the Manchus defeated Tsewang Rabtan's grandson Amursana, ending the Jungarian threat. Amursana fled to Russian Siberia, where he died of smallpox, which ravaged the Oirats as a whole. Jungaria came under Manchu rule. The last steppe empire had fallen, a victim as much of internal divisions as of Qing arms.

Qing rule was most direct over those Mongols closest to them, creating distinctions between what became Inner and Outer Mongolia. Tibetan Buddhist civilization continued to spread across Mongol society, providing a common cultural and religious identity beyond the Chinggisid imperial tradition. It was also a means to resist the pull of China, which might otherwise have assimilated them.

Some Kalmyks, increasingly unhappy with Russian interference in their internal affairs, decided in 1771 to return to Jungaria, now under Manchu rule. Those west of the Volga remained and came under closer Russian control. The rest began the arduous trek back to Xinjiang, harried by the Kazakhs and others.

The rapidly expanding Russian and Qing empires were now on either side of the Kazakhs who maneuvered between them. Dissatisfaction with Russian domination led the Kazakhs to join the rebellion of Emelian Pugachov in the mid-1770s against Catherine the Great. Sïrïm Batïr led a movement among the Kazakhs against their khans and nobles, whom he viewed as too acquiescent towards the Russians. He died in exile in Khiva, poisoned in 1797, but his movement showed that Kazakh central authority was fading. The Russians were now determining the selection of Kazakh khans.

The Kyrgyz—neighbors, allies, subjects, or enemies of various Kazakh, Uzbek and Moghulistani khans—were ruled by non-Chinggisids. The *Ta'rîkh-i Rashîdî* calls them "infidels" and "the originators of all the revolts in Moghulistan."[27] The seventeenth-century Mahmûd ibn Walî reports that they still worshipped idols, a grievous sin in Islam, and hence were "not true Muslims."[28] Islam came slowly and imperfectly to them over a long period of time. Nonetheless, they frequently involved themselves in the politics of a now-Islamic Xinjiang.

In the early sixteenth century, Ishâq Walî, a powerful Naqshbandî Sheikh, came to Altïshahr ("Six Cities": Kashghar, Khotan, Yarkand, Turfan, Yangi Hissar and Aqsu). His brother, Muhammad Yûsuf came slightly later. They claimed descent from the Prophet Muhammad. Locally, a person with such a lineage was called *khoja*, a term that also designated descendants of the first four caliphs and close companions of the Prophet Muhammad or, more mundanely, "teacher, elder, official." Subsequently, competing descendants of the "Great Master" fought among themselves for ascendancy. Muhammad Yûsuf's faction, led by his son, Hidâyat Allâh, found refuge with Galdan, the Jungarian Khan. With the Jungarian conquest of Muslim eastern Turkestan in 1678, he became governor. The rival khojas continued to feud, each faction supported by Kyrgyz tribesmen. The Qing, after destroying the Jungar Empire in 1757, initially planned to rule Kashgharia at a distance, through the khojas. Muslim resistance forced the Qing to conquer the region two years later. They made Kashgharia a tributary territory. Manchu *amban*s (high officials) were stationed in the cities and more important towns, and a military governor sat in Kulja. Substantial parts of Central Asia were under Russian or Qing rule.

CHAPTER NINE

The Problems of Modernity

In the early nineteenth century, Central Asia, politically divided and little known to outsiders, faced the weakening Qing and rapidly expanding Russian empires. British travelers, often participants in the Great Game, the Anglo-Russian rivalry in Central Asia, describe an impoverished land. Captain John Moubray Trotter, a nineteenth-century British traveler-author, commented that "not one tenth" of the amîrate of Bukhara, was "occupied by a settled population," or was "capable of cultivation." Nomads were numerous and the sands encroached on everything, leaving behind "deserted habitations."[1] Low population density heightened the impression of decline. In the mid-nineteenth century, Mongolia had about 500,000 inhabitants, disease and monasticism taking many young men out of the reproductive pool. By the early twentieth century, Russian-dominated Central Asia may have held some 11 to 12 million people. Poor living conditions produced high death rates.

Knowledge about the wider world varied. The Bukharan *Qush Begi* (prime minister) whom Alexander Burnes, a British army officer, visited for three years in the early 1830s, knew the "customs and politics of Europe" and was "well informed" about Russia.[2] The Khan of Khiva, whom another British officer, Captain Frederick G. Burnaby, in 1875 found "muy simpatico," was aware of the Anglo-Russian rivalry but was uncertain if the English and Germans were the same "nation."[3] Khiva enjoyed a reputation for lawlessness and was a notorious center of the slave trade. Military technology was poorly developed. Eugene Schuyler, an American diplomat, reported in 1873 that Khoqand had "considerable difficulty in manufacturing cartridges" for their Russian rifles and the requirements of their Russian-based artillery system "had not been thoroughly learned."[4]

The Manghït Amîrs of Bukhara, compensating for their lack of Chinggisid credentials, strictly enforced public religious observance, adding to a reputation for religious fanaticism. In reality, as Schuyler observed, "mullahs and dervishes" excepted, most people were religious only in public, but in private tended to "commit many sins, if they think no one knows it."[5] Burnes praised the tolerance and "good fellowship" of his Muslim travel companions,[6] but in Bukhara, he had to wear clothing indicating that he was a non-Muslim and could not "ride within the walls of the city," a right accorded solely to Muslims. Only certain public baths were open to non-Muslims, the *'ulama* claiming that water became "polluted" by the presence of women or non-Muslims and would turn into blood. Once-famous Bukharan schools stagnated in the rote learning of theology. Bukhara's volunteer army of 13,000 foot soldiers, 500 cavalrymen, and 620 artillery troops was poorly equipped, poorly paid, and largely engaged in other pursuits. It intimidated local inhabitants who could be arrested for venturing forth at night.

Khoqand, largest of the khanates, raided and traded with Qing China, while giving refuge to the Khojas, who preached Holy War in Xinjiang.

Sayyid Muhammad Rahîm (second from left), the heir to the Khivan throne, photographed with his companions sometime before 1896. He was a non-Chinggisid descended from Qunghrat Uzbek ïnaqs, "trusted advisors," who had taken power in the late eighteenth century. Photo by I. Voljinski, around 1895–96, Collection of Tetragon A. S.

Bukhara, Khiva, and Khoqand warred with each other, Iran and the Kazakhs. All took captives, who ended up in the Bukharan slave markets. "Three fourths" of Bukhara's populace was of "slave extraction."[7]South of the Uzbek khanates, Ahmad Durrânî Khan, a Pushtun chief from the area of Herat, used conquest and diplomacy to gather under his rule an uneasy mix of Pushtuns, Tajiks, Uzbeks, Turkmens, and Mongols, creating modern Afghanistan. The British viewed it a buffer to Russian Indian ambitions.

In the steppe, the Kazakhs, who exported about 1.5 million head of cattle and 100,000 horses annually, seeking trade and political maneuverability, became both Russian and Qing subjects. In 1801, their ever-fractious Chinggisids produced a fourth horde, under Bökey Khan, near the Volga-Ural mesopotamia. The Russian Empire was daily inching closer, the harbinger of new political and economic alignments.

Although Peter the Great's attempts to conquer Transoxiana in the early eighteenth century ended in disaster, a line of Russian forts advanced into the steppelands following the 1740 conquest of Bashkiria in the Ural region. Russia was responding to nomadic slave raids, a matter of genuine concern, but also sought to become the middleman in the overland trade. Reports of rich gold deposits in Turkestan aroused further interest.

Catherine the Great altered previously anti-Islamic policies. Her predecessor, Elizabeth, had destroyed 418 of the 536 mosques in the district of Kazan and forbade proselytizing.[8] Catherine, seeking to bring all religious institutions under greater state control, gave Muslims the status of a tolerated minority and created the Muslim Spiritual Assembly in 1788 to direct their religious life. She allowed the reopening of Muslim schools, but Muslims were wary about institutions under the control of a Christian state. Russian authorities distinguished between steppe Islam, suffused, they believed, with shamanism, and the Islam of the Uzbek cities, which they considered hotbeds of fanaticism. Catherine viewed Islam as a "civilizing" tool that would first make Kazakhs good Muslims, then good citizens, and eventually good Christians. She used Tatar teachers, her subjects, who could travel among the nomads and speak their language, to preach a more "correct" Islam. The Tatars became an important factor in implanting in the steppe an Islam that adhered more closely to traditional Muslim practices.

Between 1822 and 1848, Russia annexed all the Kazakh hordes, abolished the power of the khans, and placed the tribes under different provincial and territorial administrations. Revolts ensued, occasionally directed at Khiva and Khoqand, since some tribes were more or less under their jurisdiction. In 1853, the Russian General Perovskii took the Khoqandian fort of Aq Mechit. The Russian advance continued with few interruptions over the next three decades. Neighboring Kyrgyz tribes, goaded by Khoqandian misrule, petitioned for Russian overlordship. In 1865, General M. G. Cherniaev, encouraged by the pro-Russian attitudes of some of Tashkent's merchants and acting without government orders, took Tashkent, a Khoqandian possession. The government, not wanting to provoke the British, ever-wary of Russian encroachments on India, recalled him, gave him medals and—most significantly—kept Tashkent.

In 1868, General P. K. von Kaufman, the newly appointed governor-general of Turkestan (all the Central Asian lands taken since 1853), reduced the Khoqandian khan Khudâyâr to little more than a Russian vassal. The Amîr of Bukhara, Muzaffar ad-Dîn, facing domestic foes, his army routed, accepted a treaty. Bukhara became a Russian protectorate in June 1868, spared outright annexation only because Russia feared provoking a religious war. 'Abd al-'Azîz Sâmî, a Bukharan historian of the late nineteenth to early twentieth century, attributed Bukhara's fall to moral decay, expressed in unjust rule and fanatical *'ulama* (Islamic religious authorities). The army, he maintained, was thoroughly corrupt and largely consisted of "thieves, gamblers, drunkards, some crazy and insane, others lame or blind, who never heard a gunshot."[9] The Khanate of Khiva became a Russian protectorate in 1873. Khoqand was simply annexed in 1876. In each instance, as local chroniclers such as Sâmî make clear, the misrule and decadence of the local elites played as great a role in the fall of the khanates as the force of Russian arms. Merv (also pronounced Mary), the last Turkmen center, was annexed in 1884, bringing Russia to the borders of Iran and Afghanistan. Russian forces soon crossed into Afghanistan, much to the consternation of Britain.

Russia, like other imperialist powers, claimed it was bringing its "civilizing mission" to the benighted "natives." The Russian costs for these territorial gains, roughly equal in size to Western Europe, were relatively light. Perhaps a thousand men perished in the actual fighting. Central Asian losses were much higher. Russian generals, facing weak and divided opponents, enjoyed technological and numerical superiority. By the end of the nineteenth century, Russia had some twenty million Muslim subjects, larger than the Muslim population of the Ottoman Empire. The government was uncertain about the loyalties of its newly acquired Muslim population—as it was also of its non-Orthodox Christian and Jewish subjects.[10]

In Qing-dominated eastern Central Asia, matters unfolded somewhat differently. Inner Mongolia faced colonization by large numbers of Chinese peasants. Chinese merchants controlled the economy throughout Mongolia. Urban development was weak. Urga had perhaps 7000 inhabitants, most living in tents. A sizable minority were monks. Cultural differences, economic competition, and exploitation created enmity between Mongols and Chinese. Lamaistic Buddhism undoubtedly played a key role in preserving Mongol identity. Mongol princes north of the Gobi, and hence at some distance from direct Qing control, used the Russians as a counterpoise to China.

Sharp cultural and religious differences distinguished Muslim Xinjiang from its Qing overlords. Between 1825 and 1857 Kashgharia erupted in revolts, led by or on behalf of the Khojas, who were themselves torn by deadly factional rivalries. Choqan Valikhanov, a Kazakh scholar and Russian army officer, in 1858, described the chaos that descended on Kashghar. Qing soldiers sacked the city, seized the women, and carried out executions "with ceremonial, horrific slowness."[11] The skulls of the executed adorned the portals of the city.

Elsewhere, the situation was calmer until the 1850s. Crushing taxation and Qing misrule contributed to revolts of the Dungans (a term for Chinese Muslims), soon imitated by their Turkic coreligionists. Xinjiang dissolved into a crazy quilt of local rivalries and anti-Qing movements. As the Qing hold slipped, Ya'qûb Beg, a Khoqandian general, seized much of the region and sought diplomatic and trade relations with Russia and Britain. London recognized his "amîrate." Russia exploited the situation, taking the Ili River Valley in 1871. When Ya'qûb Beg died in 1877, his "amîrate" collapsed and the Qing, much to everyone's surprise, restored their authority. Russian-Qing territorial differences over the Ili Valley were settled in 1881. Determined to assert closer control, in 1884 the Qing gave east Turkestan and Jungaria provincial status. Henceforth, the province of Xinjiang ("new frontier") was to be directly administered by Qing officials.

The Russians had no master plan for the administration of their newly won Central Asian domain. In the General Governorates, the population remained under traditional leaders. Russian administration operated, as far as possible, at a distance, hoping to lessen the cost of governance and the chances for friction with local Islamic sensibilities. General von Kaufman maintained that Islam should be ignored and that, lacking state support, it would wither away. The calculation that the seemingly less devout nomads would become Russified and eventually Christianized proved erroneous. By the latter half of the nineteenth

The core territories, reorganized in 1898, consisted of two General Governorates: the Steppe (consisting of the provinces of Akmolinsk and Semipalatinsk) and Turkestan (comprising the provinces of Syr Darya, Semirech'e, Fergana, Samarkand, and Transcaspia) as well as the two protectorates of Bukhara and Khiva. The General Governorate of Orenburg administered the rest of the steppe zone of Kazakhstan (Ural'sk and Turgay provinces).

century the role of Islam in Kazakh life grew, becoming one of their important sources of identity.

The Russians sought to keep Central Asians divided and isolated from "harmful" modernizing ideas such as democracy. Unlike other ethnically non-Russian subjects, they could not be drafted into the army—where they might also acquire knowledge of modern warfare and weaponry. Hoping to prevent change, tsarist autocracy often made common cause with the more conservative elites and 'ulama. The latter even resisted attempts at improving public hygiene and sanitation because they came from nonbelievers. These policies perpetuated backwardness.

Russia sought to extract natural resources and keep the "natives" quiet. Russians and others from the European regions of the Russian empire, largely officials and skilled workers, settled in cities that often grew up around older "native" towns. Von Kaufman wanted administrators who knew local languages and customs. Teams of scientists, ethnographers, and artists arrived to catalogue "natives," flora, and fauna. Sorting out the various groupings was a difficult task but one that was essential for imperial administration. Individuals often had multi-layered identities of religion, clan, tribe, and ethnic group, and they answered inquiries according to how they perceived the affiliations of the questioner.

The newly conquered and annexed peoples were designated *inorodtsy* (aliens), subjects but not citizens of Russia. Tsarist policy retained Islamic Sharî'ah and customary law, *'Adat*—as long as they did not contravene government policies. In the General Governorate of Turkestan, with its long history of urban Islam, the government continued its policy of benign neglect in religious affairs. Nonetheless, revolts against Russian rule began to occur after 1885—usually under Sûfî leadership. In the General Governorate of the Steppe, however, the state financed and attempted to manage Muslim institutions. While trying to make the nomads reliable taxpayers and encouraging their settlement, the government steadily encroached on their best pasturages. It opened these "state" lands to agricultural colonists, mainly Cossacks, Russians, and Ukrainians, but also groups from Xinjiang: the Taranchi and Chinese Muslims. Mass colonization began in the 1890s. Between 1896 and 1916, more than one million colonists took one-fifth of the land. By 1914, Russians constituted 30 to 40 percent of the population of Kazakhstan. Turkestan received some 336,000 settlers in 1916 alone.

As the worldwide demand for cotton grew, Turkestan with its long history of cotton cultivation became "a huge cotton plantation for Russia."[12] By 1912, it produced 64 percent of Russian cotton. Central Asia's increasingly one-crop economy made it dependent on global price fluctuations. Industrialization forced traditional craftsmen and artisans into unequal competition with machine-made goods. The grip of the tsarist government tightened with Central Asia's growing economic importance. The railroads brought the global economy directly to Central Asia, stimulating urban growth. Tashkent grew from 120,000 inhabitants in 1877 (according to Eugene Schuyler) to 234, 000 in the Russian census of 1910.[13] Foreign observers credited the Russians with providing more security than had previously been known. Expanding contacts with Russia and modernizing Muslims (the Volga Tatars) were recasting Central Asia's cultural and intellectual world. Traditional leaders who had not adjusted to the new order faded.

Reform and renewal in Central Asia was part of a larger Muslim revival and reaction to the threat of Europe. It advanced through several stages, religious and cultural renewal, educational reform, and finally the emergence of national consciousness: nationalism. There were different currents of change. The Salafiyya movement (Arabic *salaf*, "forefather") stressed a return to the values and practices of the early Muslims—often interpreted as a fundamentalist rejection of all innovations. Others argued that Muslims would have to acquire modern technology and fashion a culture that could both accommodate traditional religious and social values while at the same time fully function in the industrial world. That meant a modern, secular education. In Central Asia, as elsewhere in the Muslim world, schools had been religious in orientation.

In Turkestan, von Kaufman's policy of benign neglect hoped that an ignored Muslim educational system would simply disappear. A few bilingual schools for resident Russians and the indigenous peoples were opened in 1876 and largely shunned by Muslims, wary of their intentions. By 1894, 95 percent of the students of the 90 bilingual schools were Russians. Among the Tatars and the Kazakhs who already had direct contact with modernizing ideas flowing from Russia, the situation was different. In the 1850s, a few schools for Kazakhs had opened, in part to lessen previously encouraged Islamic influences from the Tatars. In 1870, the government founded Russo-Tatar schools, emphasizing secular education. This coincided with reform movements initiated by the Tatars themselves.

The Tatars valued education highly and had an extensive religious school system attached to their mosques where *imâm*s (prayer leaders) taught boys reading, the Qur'ân, the tenets of Islam, Arabic, Persian, and arithmetic. Girls might acquire some learning from the imâm's wife. The roots of reform went deep, going back to Gabdennasïr ('Abd al-Nasr) al-Kursavî, who urged Muslims to study the Qur'ân and use their own judgment to create new interpretations to meet modern challenges. The educator and reformer Shihâbaddîn Marjânî argued that becoming more modern would bring Muslims closer to the Islam of the forefathers.

A Crimean Tatar journalist, reformer, and social activist, Ismâ'îl Bey Gaspïralï (Russian: Gasprinskii), promoted the *Usûl-i Jadîd* (new method) schools, a reaction to traditional rote learning. The new method consisted of using a phonetic rather than the traditional syllabic system to teach reading. More radically, he separated the schools from the mosque-madrasa complex and used specially trained teachers for the primary schools. Girls had their own schools. Instruction was systematized with appropriate textbooks for each grade. Gaspïralï's newspaper, *Terjümân* (Translator), which appeared in 1883, advocated cultural reform and the unity of the Turkic peoples. *Jadîdism*, underway in Kazan by the 1880s, came to Turkestan in the following decade.

These modest reforms provoked vicious attacks from adherents of the *usûl-i qadîm* (old method), who feared that they would lead to assimilation and apostasy. The government, uncertain of Jadidism's political goals, neither supported nor actively opposed the new schools. Ultimately, wealthy Tatar merchants provided funding. Tatar interest in education was reflected in a literacy rate (20.4 percent) that surpassed that of the Russians (18.3 percent).

By the eve of World War I, there were some 5000 Jadid schools in the Russian Empire. The tsarist government, wary of Jadidism among Tatars, viewed it as an antidote to "Muslim fanaticism" in Bukhara. The amîr suppressed the Jadidist *Yâsh Bukhârâliqlar* (Young Bukharans) in 1910 and many fled to the Ottoman Empire, including Abdurrauf Fitrat, later one of the revolutionary intellectual luminaries of Uzbekistan. The key theme of the movement was that Muslims would remain powerless as long as they did not possess modern knowledge.

The Jadidist educational and cultural reforms were the necessary precursors to national movements. Modern national identities build on notions of a shared language, culture, and territory. Most settled Central Asians thought of their birthplace and its immediate environs as their homeland. Nomadic populations most strongly identified with clan and tribe. Many Muslims still saw their primary identity in religious terms. The Tatars and Kazakhs, geographically closest to the Russians, were the first to begin to perceive themselves as distinct national entities. The Tatar Qayyûm Nâsîrî and the Kazakh Ibrâhîm Altïnsarin pioneered national languages, crucial to the development of national movements.

Defeat in the Russo-Japanese War (1904–05) sparked the revolution of 1905 in Russia. The war demonstrated that a modernized non-European people could defeat a European power, encouraging revolutionary movements in the Ottoman Empire and Iran, which had been losing land to Russia for more than a century. The weakened tsarist autocracy briefly opened up political life, permitting a representative assembly, the *Duma*. Four Dumas, which included Muslim participation, met between 1906 and 1914, but were unable to overcome tsarist resistance to reform. Nonetheless, participation had an impact on the modernizing intellectuals in Bukhara. If representative government could be achieved in autocratic Russia, then similar reforms in Bukhara were conceivable. The Muslims of the empire held a series of congresses to formulate a united program of action to press their political demands. They broke into factions. The *Ittifâq al-Muslimîn* (Union of Muslims) called for freedom of religion, regional autonomy, and a liberal, constitutional monarchy, like the Russian Constitutional Party (Kadets) with whom they were allied. On the left, the *Tangchilar*, men associated with the Tatar newspaper, *Tang* (Dawn), favored a non-Marxist democratic socialism. On the right were the traditional religious conservatives who had the tacit support of the tsarist government.

The strains of World War I (1914–18) broke the Russian empire. A major revolt erupted in July 1916 in Central Asia, provoked by the conscription of local peoples into labor battalions. It reflected the long-simmering anger over colonial policies, especially the influx of Russian settlers who took the best land. The government responded with harsh reprisals and armed bands of settlers engaged in massacres. Some 200,000 Central Asians perished. The February Revolution of 1917 toppled the tsar and brought a moderate, democratically inclined but fragile Provisional Government to power. The Communists (Bolsheviks) exploited Prime Minister Alexander F. Kerenskii's unwillingness to pull Russia out of the war and the deteriorating domestic situation to stage the October 1917 Revolution. Civil war followed, complicated by foreign intervention. The Bolsheviks won, retaining much of the old empire.

The Central Asian leadership tended to see political issues in national or ethno-religious terms. Many favored some kind of relationship with Russia, calling for either a distinct Muslim voice in government or various forms of autonomy. The Provisional Government willingly granted Muslims individual rights, but balked at the notion of group rights or a federal solution of this type. The Muslims themselves were divided by region and national groupings. The Kazakhs founded the Alash Orda political party in March 1917 to defend those who felt threatened by Russian colonization and Tatar cultural influence. During the civil war, they initially favored the anti-communist White forces and then switched to the Bolsheviks in November, 1919. The Bashkirs, fearful of Tatar domination in the Idel-Ural (Volga-Ural) republic that Tatar Communists were proposing, opted for their own Autonomous Bashkir Republic. The Turkestan Muslim political groups tended to be in tune with the Kadets and the Provisional Government, although smaller socialist groups also existed. The creation of a common program was probably impossible given the differences in language and local culture of the Muslim peoples. Many of the Russians in the Central Asian cities were largely socialist of one kind or another in their political orientation. They tended to view the local Muslims as political and ethnic enemies.

A particular Muslim Communist perspective emerged during the Civil War. The Tatar Bolshevik, Mirsaid Sultan Galiev, a schoolteacher turned revolutionary, viewing Russia's Muslims as a distinct people, argued that all Muslims (and indeed all non-Europeans) were, in effect, an oppressed people, the equivalent of the oppressed workers and peasants of European societies. Hence, class warfare was for the Muslim East the struggle of an oppressed Muslim people against the European imperialist-colonialist forces. He further argued that the victory of socialism among Russia's Muslims would be a springboard for revolution throughout the colonial world. Many Jadidists accepted this idea and joined the Bolsheviks. In 1918 Bolshevik rule came to Central Asia, creating the Turkestan Autonomous Soviet Socialist Republic, which overcame local and anti-Bolshevik White Guard challenges in 1919. Many local Bolsheviks still harbored ethnic prejudices. Moscow had to force them to make a place for indigenous Muslim Communists. In the Kazakh steppes the years of turmoil produced a massive famine in which as many as a million people may have died.

By 1923, the Bolsheviks consolidated control in Central Asia. The *Basmachi*, rural resistance bands, continued well into the decade. Between 1920 and 1924, the Kazakh, Turkmen, and Uzbek Soviet Socialist Republics were created. Following this National Delimitation of the Central Asian Republics, Bukhara and Khiva were formally brought into the Soviet Union in 1924, as part of the Uzbek SSR. The name "Turkestan" had to be removed. Although "Turkestanians" shared a common history, religion (Islam), and literary languages (Chaghatay and Persian/Tajik), the fundamentals for a modern sense of nationhood, the notion of "Turkestan" had too many Pan-Turkic associations. The creation of smaller "Soviet republics" with a strong Turkic character was a concession to the indigenous reformers and Jadidists, giving them space in which to develop Turkic cultures—under Soviet guidance. In 1929, the Tajik SSR was carved out of the Uzbek SSR, and in 1936 Kyrgyzstan, previously an autonomous province and then an Autonomous Soviet Socialist Republic, became the Kirgiz SSR.

The shaping of new republics and nations, encompassing somewhat less than 14 million Central Asians, largely took place during the Soviet New Economic Policy (NEP, 1921–28), which reintroduced elements of free enterprise in an effort to deal with famine and the shortage of goods. Previously, Central Asian states had centered on a dynasty rather than a "nationality." The USSR created nation-states, shaping borders to suit its own governing purposes. Every nationality was to have its own territory. The first casualties of this policy were the national communists such as Mirsaid Sultan Galiev, whose ideas were considered contrary to Marxist "principles of proletarian unity," which viewed the working class as a single unit, undivided by ethnic or religious differences. Sultan Galiev was twice arrested and is presumed to have perished in the Soviet Gulag, the system of penal labor camps in which political dissidents and criminals were imprisoned.

This 1977 Soviet poster and its smiling woman proudly proclaim: "Cotton is our happiness." In reality, Central Asia was largely transformed into a one-crop (cotton) plantation by the Soviet government. The overuse of fertilizers poisoned the soil and caused horrific birth defects to appear in some areas. Hoover Institution, Stanford University, Hoover Political Poster Collection, RU/SU 2257.12

The Soviet government then tailored nationalities for the national republics. Few Central Asians, other than modernizers, had a sense of "nationality." The region's complex ethnic structure made the problem even more daunting. All of the Soviet national "delimitations" were arbitrary political decisions, rationalized by ethnographic and linguistic studies. In this regard, Soviet policy must be viewed as a massive—and largely successful—project of social and ethnic engineering. Language became one of the critical markers of Soviet identity.[14] As a consequence, the origins of the modern languages of the region, their formation, affiliations, and connections have become issues with important political consequences.

Uzbekistan, the most populous of the Soviet Central Asian republics, gave local intellectuals inclined towards Pan-Turkism a large, Turkic state of their own. *Uzbek*, however, would replace *Türk* or *Türkî*, terms that were current. They hinted at Pan-Turkism and Turkey, which was undergoing its own political and cultural revolutions, one closely observed by Central Asian Turkic intellectuals. The use of Uzbek to designate peoples who had not previously used this term for themselves, and the insistence on the Turkic character of a population that had a long history of bilingualism in Turkic and Persian-Tajik, was a means of winning over Jadidists and other reformers. The term *Sart*, denoting groupings of Tajik origin that had become Turkicized or various Turkic groups that had sedentarized, almost half of the population of Uzbekistan, disappeared as an identity in the 1926 census.

All, regardless of their linguistic and other distinctive features, were now officially *Uzbeks*, for some an identity that did not come naturally. Uzbekistan contained Bukhara and Samarkand two cities whose populations were predominantly Tajik, albeit bilingual. *Tajiks*, a term used disparagingly by some Turkic-speakers for mountain peoples, many of whom were Shi'ites who spoke other Iranian tongues, as well as for Tajik-speakers, demanded their own republic. Some defined it in ways that would have shrunk Uzbekistan and made Tajikistan the largest Soviet Central Asian republic. Debates over this issue raged during the latter half of the 1920s. The Soviets exploited this ethnic rivalry to lessen the veiled but still Pan-Turkist aspirations of some Uzbek intellectuals.[15]

In time, Soviet policies produced a distinct sense of national identity among the Uzbeks, Tajiks, and others. Older distinctions of clan and region survived in the factional groupings (often with an ideological veneer) that frequently competed for power in both Soviet and post-Soviet Central Asia. Tribal identity is still a factor in Turkmenistan and

Kyrgyzstan and among some older Uzbeks. In Kazakhstan, Great, Middle, and Little Horde affiliations continue to shape competing political factions.

Each new nationality required its own history, distinguishing it from its neighbors (often closely related peoples with shared histories) as well as its own literature, folklore, and, of course, language and alphabet. Politicians and scholars convened to sort out these questions and selected certain dialects as national literary languages, buttressing political needs with scholarly rationalizations. Most Turkic languages used the Arabic alphabet, which blurred the pronunciation differences between them. Turkmen *göz,* Kazakh *köz,* and Tatar *küz* (eye) were written identically. Although orthographic reform was already part of pre-revolutionary modernizing projects, there were pressures to replace the Arabic script. It linked Soviet Muslims with Muslim populations in neighboring lands—a source of potential subversion. In 1927 and 1928, Kyrgyz, Uzbek, Turkmen, Kazakh, and Qara Qalpaq adopted the Latin script. Turkey did the same in 1928. Tajik followed not long after. In the late 1930s, the Soviet government decided that Cyrillic should replace Latin, a process completed by 1942. Russian became a required subject in all non-Russian schools. The goal was the *sblizhenie* (bringing together) of the 126 different nationalities of the Soviet Union. Ultimately, this would produce their *sliianie* ("melding together") into a new "Soviet Person" who would almost certainly be Russian speaking.

The enormous strains of collectivization and sedentarization of the nomads, which ended private farming and private herds, completed by the late 1930s, transformed society, but at tremendous cost. In Kazakhstan perhaps one million people perished, as did millions in Ukraine. Purges killed off indigenous political leaders.

The new Soviet culture was expressed in the local languages, but its contents were determined by Moscow. Russians, or other non-Central Asians, controlled the republic Communist Parties. Token representatives of the indigenous peoples received second or lower-ranking positions. Muslim schools were closed by the late 1920s and 1930s, along with Islamic courts and the Muslim Spiritual Assembly. Islam was portrayed as backward and, like Christianity, Judaism, and Buddhism, considered inimical to the atheistic ideology of the new state. "Militant atheism" was downplayed during World War II when the USSR was fighting for its existence. The government sought to rally Muslims by reviving a sovietized variant of the Muslim Spiritual Assembly in 1943. Several *madrasa*s were opened. Its officials, like those of other officially recognized religions, were carefully monitored.

There were significant social changes. Mass education was introduced with some success. In 1927, Moscow mandated the liberation of Central Asian women, undertaking campaigns against veiling and female seclusion in Uzbekistan. In reality, these practices were not universal, and Jadidist and other local reformers had long called for such changes. Soviet policies, which invaded very personal territory, produced a reaction. Folk Islam and traditions, such as veiling, a practice that varied from region to region, and male circumcision became symbols of identity. Moscow ultimately prevailed with regard to the veil. Women gained full legal equality with men and equal career opportunities. Some women pursued this; many, especially in the rural areas, did not or could not. Russians and Central Asians worked side by side, especially in the cities, but intermarriage was rare.

By the late 1950s, improving living standards produced a substantial demographic upswing. Soviet Russian culture remained dominant, but accorded more latitude in expression to local cultures. The fictionalized biography of the Kazakh modernizer Abay Qunanbayuli (Russian: Kunanbaev) by the novelist Mukhtar Auezov introduced Soviet audiences to the richness of Kazakh nomadic culture, while pressing themes acceptable to the administration. Major novelists, such as the Kyrgyz Chingiz Aitmatov, whose *The Day Lasts more than a Hundred Years* (1980) encapsulates the experiences of the Kyrgyz under Soviet rule, appeared in both Kyrgyz and Russian, to local and international acclaim.

By the 1970s, the central government felt more at ease in turning over leadership in the Central Asian republics to "natives," usually with a Russian theoretically his subordinate in the local government and party hierarchy, but actually there to watch Moscow's interests. During the "stagnation" and growing corruption that typified much of the era in which Leonid Brezhnev led the USSR (1964–82), this indigenous leadership became a real force with which Moscow had to negotiate. Anti-Soviet sentiments were more openly expressed in the late 1980s, the age of *glasnost'* (freedom of expression) ushered in by Mikhail Gorbachev, Brezhnev's ultimate successor and the last Communist ruler. In December 1991, the Soviet Union was disbanded and reorganized into a loose union termed the Commonwealth of Independent States (with the exception of Georgia and the Baltic states of Lithuania, Latvia, and Estonia).

In the aftermath of the Soviet Union's collapse, Central Asians, under authoritarian regimes of varying severity that came to power in late Soviet times, found themselves on the threshold of a new era. They now face enormous problems. Pollution has left a legacy of disease and ecological disaster. There is the prospect of great wealth (oil, gas, and other natural resources), but uncertainty as to how to exploit it.

National identities established by the Soviets continue, but are being infused with new content. Tamerlane, whose descendants were driven out of Transoxiana by the Uzbeks, has become a symbol of Uzbek identity. The Uzbek leadership wants association with the image of a powerful conqueror and major figure on the world stage. It also wants to put some distance between Uzbekistan and Kazakhstan, in effect continuing Soviet policy.[16] National, ethnic and regional rivalries remain unresolved. Indeed, even the long-standing, but occasionally tense, symbiosis of Uzbek and Tajik has been undergoing severe strains. Tajiks in Uzbekistan claim discrimination. In some regions, there is the threat of radical Islamic movements, usually termed "Wahhâbis" after the name of the conservative Sunnî sect dominant in Saudi Arabia. The Saudis have often provided the funds for Islamic revival movements. In Uzbekistan and elsewhere, some of these groups have engaged in violent opposition to the current governments and have joined the Taliban or al-Qaeda.[17]

Language remains a critical component of identity. Many Central Asian states have sought to "purify" their language by ridding them of Russian terms. Some have changed alphabets. In 1991, Turkmenistan, like Azerbaijan in Transcaucasia, adopted a Latin alphabet largely modeled on that of Modern Turkish, a close relative. In Uzbekistan, a "reformed" Latin-based alphabet appeared in 1995,[18] but books continue to be published in Cyrillic.

Most of the current leaders have practiced varying degrees of political repression, familiar to them from the Soviet system in which they were raised. Saparmurat Niyazov, leader of Turkmenistan from 1990 until his death in 2006, declared himself *Türkmenbashï*, "Leader of the Turkmen." His extravagant personality cult accompanied a repressive regime. The less flamboyant Uzbek president, Islam Karimov, has been equally intolerant of political opposition. Nursultan Nazarbayev, who became the president of Kazakhstan in 1991, has been more effective in promoting economic growth without overt political oppression. Oil and mineral wealth accounted for 80 percent of earnings, but 40 percent of the population lived in poverty in 2008.[19] Desertification is claiming once fertile pastures in Turkmenistan and Kazakhstan. Kyrgyzstan has a fragile democracy torn by factional strife. Tajikistan's civil war (1992–97) pitting reformers against Islamists, often with strong undercurrents of regional and ethnic factionalism, left the country in ruins.

After the Chinese Revolution of 1911, a series of warlords replaced Qing rule in Xinjiang. They held power, while fending off encroachments from Russia/USSR and the Chinese Republican government. All of them faced unrest from the local Turkic Muslims. In 1921, a group of east Turkestani intellectuals meeting in Tashkent revived the Uighur name (unused for centuries) and began to promote Uighur nationalism. The majority of the settled Turkî-speaking population adopted this common designation. Uighur uprisings produced the East Turkestan Republic in 1944 under Uighur leadership, while Chiang Kai-shek's Chinese Nationalist government was distracted by war with Japan and the struggle with the Chinese Communists. In 1949, the Communists, victors in the Chinese civil war, dismantled it. They suppressed Uighur nationalism and rewrote the history of Xinjiang, portraying it as an ancient possession of China. Periodic attempts were made to more closely integrate the region and its diverse, non-Chinese population into China proper.

During the Cultural Revolution in the 1960s and '70s, large numbers of Chinese were settled there, putting the demographic dominance of the local Muslim peoples in jeopardy. In 1949, there were 300,000 Chinese in Xinjiang. Today, 7.5 million Chinese constitute 40 percent of the population while the 8.5 million Uighurs form 45 percent.[20] Cognizant of these concerns, the government has exempted the Uighurs and other national minorities from its one child per family policy. Newspapers and books are published in the local languages. Uighurs use the Arabic script, which separates them from Turkic-speaking post-Soviet Central Asia. An increasing number of the younger generation knows Chinese, essential to full participation in the life of the country, but they are a minority. Uighur resistance and separatist movements have developed. Some of them, such as the East Turkestan Islamic Movement, have adopted violent tactics and are considered terrorist organizations with possible ties to al-Qaeda.

Inner Mongolia remained within the Chinese orbit after 1911. Chinese economic and demographic pressure continued. Although united by language and a historical consciousness largely based on the Chinggisid Empire, Mongol nationalists were divided by region. Prince Demchukdongrob, a nationalist leader, had hoped to gain autonomy within China in return for cooperation against the Japanese. When this policy failed, the local aristocracy, seeking Japanese support for their conquest of Outer Mongolia, cooperated with Japan, which had established itself in neighboring Manchuria in 1931. Inner Mongolia remains under Chinese rule.

Outer Mongolia, caught between Russia and China, retained an uneasy independence during the twentieth century. It declared the eighth Jebtsundamba Khutukhtu, Bogdo Khan, the ruler of independent Mongolia in 1911. Russia backed him, but declined to support plans to include Inner Mongolia and other Mongol territories in this state. In 1913, China, while retaining its nominal sovereignty, agreed to Outer Mongolian self-rule. The Treaty of Kiakhta (1915) between Russia, China, and the Mongols confirmed Mongolia's autonomous (de facto independent) status. China, taking advantage of the Russian Civil War, reasserted its claims and retook the country in 1919–20. Sükhe Bator, a young revolutionary, reclaimed Mongol independence in 1921 and established the People's Government of Mongolia. When Bogdo Khan died in 1924, the monarchy was abolished and the Mongol People's Republic (MPR) was declared, based on Soviet models. China remained its nominal overlord, while the MPR drew closer to Moscow. Internal policies, such as collectivization and political purges, mirrored those of the USSR. Choibalsan, the army chief, ultimately emerged as the dominant figure.

The Japanese threat produced a treaty of alliance with the USSR in 1936. Three years later, a joint Soviet-Mongol army defeated Japanese forces in a series of engagements in the ill-defined borderlands. When the USSR declared war on Japan on August 8, 1945, the MPR followed two days later.

After the close of World War II, a national plebiscite (1945) confirmed Mongolian independence, subsequently reconfirmed by China and the USSR. Under the premiership of Tsedenbal, who came to power after Choibalsan's death in 1952 Mongolia, still concerned about China's ultimate goals, remained a Soviet satellite state until the fall of the Soviet Union. In 1991, it changed its name to the Republic of Mongolia and has since become a multiparty democracy. Its population of 2.5 million face enormous problems of economic underdevelopment. Pasturelands account for 75 percent of Mongolia's landmass, but pastoral nomadism, the dominant industry, faces an uncertain future in the modern world economy. Chinggis Khan, whose name appears on everything from vodka and beer labels to rock bands, remains a potent national symbol.

Pronunciation Guide

Diacritics for long vowels in place-names have been omitted, for example, Bukhara instead of Bukhârâ. They have been retained for personal names and titles, for example, Khwarazm is used for the city and country, but Khwârazmshâh for the title of the ruler.

The following is a simplified guide for English speakers.

VOWELS

Sound	Example in English
â in Arabic	A as in dad except when preceded by ḍ, ṣ, ṭ or ẓ, when it is more like A as in father
â in Persian	AW
î	EE as in sweet
ï	I as in igloo
ö	U as in urge
û	OO as in tooth
ü	EW as in dew

CONSONANTS

Sound	Example in English	Other information
' is the Arabic 'ain		a brief pause before a vowel
dh in Arabic	TH as in "this"	
gh in Arabic, Persian, Turkic, and Mongol	G as in gorilla, but from deeper in the throat	a guttural hard "g"
kh in Arabic, Persian, and Mongol	CH in "Loch Ness"	a guttural CH sound
q in Arabic, Persian, Turkic, and Classical Mongol		"k" pronounced deep in the throat

Chronology

CA. 38000 BCE
Humans enter Central Asia

CA. 6000 BCE
Development of agriculture

CA. 4800 BCE
Domestication of the horse

CA. 3000 BCE
Building of irrigation canals in Central Asia

CA. 2000 BCE
Wheeled carts, chariots, emergence of pastoral nomadism

CA. 1500 or 1200
Birth of Zoroaster (perhaps as late as 600 BCE)

CA. 1000 BCE
Appearance of the composite bow in Central Asia; emergence of mounted, organized armed groups

CA. 700 BCE
Scythian-Saka tribes in Pontic steppes and Central Asia

556–330 BCE
Achaemenid Empire

CA. 308–128 BCE
Graeco-Bactrian Empire

CA. 209 BCE–155 CE
Xiongnu state dominates eastern Central Asia

202 BCE–220 CE
Han dynasty rules in China

CA. first century BCE to first century CE
Rise of the Kushan dynasty

CA. 230s to 270s
Fall of the Kushan Empire to the Sasanids

CA. 226–651 CE
Sasanid Empire

375
Huns cross the Volga River

Mid-fifth century
CA. 450
Emergence of Hephthalite state in Afghanistan and neighboring areas

142

453
Death of Attila

552
Rise of First Türk Qaghanate

557—CA. 567
Türks and Persians destroy Hephthalite state

630
Fall of First Türk Qaghanate in east

CA. 630–650
Khazar Qaghanate forms in western steppes

651
Arabs complete conquest of Persia, begin advance into Central Asia

659
Fall of First Türk Qaghanate in west

682–742
Reign of the Second Türk Qaghanate in the east

750
'Abbâsids overthrow Umayyads

751
Battle of the Talas

744–840
Reign of the Uighur Qaghanate

766
Western Türk Qaghanate falls to Qarluqs

770s
Oghuz tribal union migrates from Mongolia to Syr Darya region, Kimek Qaghanate forms in western Siberia

819–1005
Sâmânid dynasty in Transoxiana and eastern Iran

916–1125
Qitan (Liao) Empire in Mongolia, Manchuria and northern China

920s
Volga Bulghars convert to Islam

960
Large-scale conversion of Turkic tribes in Central Asia to Islam

965–969
Fall of Khazaria

977–1186
Reign of the Ghaznavid state in eastern Iran, Afghanistan, and northwestern India

992–1212
Reign of the Qarakhanid state in western and eastern Turkistan

1124
Yelu Dashi founds the Qara Khitai Empire (1124–1213)

1200–1221
Reign of Muhammad Khwârazmshâh

1206
Temüjin elected as Chinggis Khan

1218–1220
Mongols conquer Central Asia

1227
Death of Chinggis Khan; Mongol realm subdivides into *ulus*es (appanages) led by the four sons of Chinggis Khan—Jochi, Chaghadai, Ögödei and Tolui—and their descendants

1229–1241
Reign of Ögödei as Great Qaghan

1240
Mongols complete conquest of Rus,' Qïpchaqs, and Volga Bulgharia

1241
Mongols invade Hungary and Poland, defeat Polish and German knights at Legnica

1243
Mongols defeat Seljuks of Rûm at Köse Dagh

1251–1259
Möngke, son of Tolui, reigns as Great Qaghan

1256–1353
Iran-Iraq and much of Anatolia ruled by the Il-khânate of the Hülegüids

1258
Mongols conquer Baghdad

1260
Mamlûks defeat Mongol forces at 'Ayn Jalût in Palestine

1260–1294
Qubilai Khan, son of Möngke, reigns as Great Qaghan

1279
Mongols complete conquest of China

1313–1341
Özbek Khan of Jochid Ulus converts to Islam

1348
Outbreak of Bubonic plague

1368
End of Yuan (Mongol) rule in China

1370–1405
Dominance of Chinggisid world by Temür (Tamerlane)

1438–1455
Oirats under Esen dominate Mongols, extending their power from Manchuria to eastern Turkestan

1443–1466
Chinggisid Khanates of Crimea, Kazan, and Astrakhan are established

1451
Chinggisid Abu'l-Khayr Khan emerges as leader of Uzbeks

1501
Safavids begin conquest of Iran

1502
Collapse of the Great Horde (Golden Horde); early to mid-sixteenth-century Kazakhs divide into Great Horde, Middle Horde, Little Horde; Khojas are established in eastern Turkistan

1526
Babur, having fled Uzbeks, founds Mughal Empire in South Asia

1552–1556
Moscow conquers Kazan and Astrakhan

1578
Altan Khan, Mongol leader, gives title *Dalai Lama* to Tibetan Gelugpa leader Sonam Gyatso; Buddhism spreads rapidly among Mongols

1616
Nurhaci, a Jurchen chieftain, proclaims himself khan

1620
Oirats convert to Buddhism

1635
Abahai, Nurhaci's son, adopts name *Manchu* for his people

1644
Manchus conquer China, founding the Qing dynasty

1648
Lamasery founded at Urga (today Ulan Bator)

1650
Formation of Kalmyk state on lower Volga

1676–1697
Reign of Galdan Khan of the Junghar Empire

1689
Treaty of Nerchinsk establishes borders between Russian and Qing Empires

1697–1727
Reign of Tsewang Rabtan of the Junghar Empire

1709
Foundation of Khoqand Khanate

1727
Treaty of Kiakhta stabilizes Russian and Qing borders and commercial relations

1731–1742
Kazakhs accept Russian protection

1753
Manghït *Atalïq*s become *Amîrs* of Bukhara

1757–1759
Qing end Junghar Empire, conquer Eastern Turkistan

1822–1848
Russia annexes the Kazakh hordes

1865–1884
Russian conquest of Central Asia

1883–1884
Qing restore authority in eastern Turkistan, rename it Xinjiang (New Frontier Province)

1890s
Russian colonization of Central Asia, in particular Kazakhstan

1905
Japan defeats Russia in Russo-Japanese War; Russian Revolution of 1905

1911
Overthrow of Qing dynasty; Outer Mongolia declares itself independent under Bogdo Khan

1917
February Revolution in Russia, followed by Bolshevik Revolution in October 1917

1918–1921
Russian Civil War

1919–1920
China retakes Outer Mongolia

1921
East Turkestani intellectuals meeting in Tashkent, revive "Uighur" as the national name for the Turkî-speaking Muslim population of East Turkistan; Sükhe Bator reestablishes independence of Outer Mongolia

1923
Bolshevik control of Russian Central Asia complete

1924
Bukhara and the Khwarazmian Republic brought into the Soviet Union; National Delimitation creates boundaries of the Soviet Central Asian republics; death of Bogdo Khan; establishment of Mongol People's Republic

1927–1928
Kyrgyz, Uzbek, Türkmen, Kazakh, and Qara Qalpaq switch from Arabic to Latin script

1930s–1942
Türkic languages switch to Cyrillic script

1944–1949
An independent republic is established in East Turkestan

1991
Soviet Union collapses; Commonwealth of Independent States, which included formerly Soviet Central Asian republics, forms; Mongol People's Republic, long a Soviet satellite, declares its independence as the Republic of Mongolia

Notes

INTRODUCTION

1. Also written "Turkistan." *Turkistân* is a Persian word meaning "country of the Turks."

2. Sir Aurel Stein, *Ruins of Desert Cathay* vol. 1(1912; repr. New York: Dover, 1987) 393.

3. Ruth I. Meserve, "The Inhospitable Land of the Barbarians," *Journal of Asian History* 16 no. 1 (1982) : 51–89.

4. Richard N. Frye, *The Heritage of Persia* (Cleveland-New York: World Publishing, 1963) 38–39.

5. John K. Fairbank, "A Preliminary Framework" in *The Chinese World Order*, ed. J. K. Fairbank (Cambridge, MA: Harvard University Press, 1970), 9–10; Lien-sheng Yang, "Historical Notes on the Chinese World Order" in Fairbank, *The Chinese World Order*, 20–22; Christopher I. Beckwith, *Empires of the Silk Road* (Princeton: Princeton University Press, 2009), xxi–xxv, 320–362. Marc S. Abramson, *Ethnic Identity in Tang China* (Philadelphia: University of Pennsylvania Press, 2008) thoroughly explores the complexities of Chinese notions of ethnic boundaries.

6. Vladimir N. Basilov, *Nomads of Eurasia*, trans. Mary F. Zirin (Seattle: Natural History Museum of Los Angeles Country in association with University of Washington Press, 1989), 23–26. On Scythian attire, see S. A. Iatsenko, *Kostium drevnei Evrazii. Iranoiazychnye narody* (Moscow: Vostochnaia Literatura, 2006), 47–102. On the "Golden Man" as "Golden Woman," see Jeannine Davis-Kimball with Mona Behan, *Warrior Women: An Archaeologist's Search for History's Hidden Heroines* (New York: Warner Books, 2002), 96–107.

7. Tsagan Törbat et al., "A Rock Tomb of the Ancient Turkic Period in the Zhargalant Khairkhan Mountains, Khovd Aimag, with the Oldest Preserved Horse-Head Fiddle in Mongolia-A Preliminary Report" *Bonn Contributions to Asian Archaeology* 4 (2009), 373–374.

8. David Anthony, *The Horse, The Wheel, and Language* (Princeton: Princeton University Press, 2007), 5, 11–13, 41–42, 46–59, 81–84, 99–101; J. P. Mallory and D. Q. Adams, *The Oxford Introduction to Proto-Indo-European and the Proto-Indo-European World* (Oxford: Oxford University Press, 2006), 442–463.

9. Alexander Vovin, "The End of the Altaic Controversy" *Central Asiatic Journal* 49 no. 1 (2005), 71–132; Christopher I. Beckwith, *Koguryo: The Language of Japan's Continental Relatives* (Leiden: Brill, 2004), 164–165, 184–194.

CHAPTER 1

1. David W. Anthony, *The Horse, the Wheel, and Language: How Bronze-Age Riders from the Eurasian Steppes Shaped the World* (Princeton: Princeton University Press, 2007), 191–192, 200, 211.

2. Anthony, *The Horse*, 221–224, 460–462; Robert Drews, *Early Riders: The Beginnings of Mounted Warfare in Asia and Europe* (New York: Routledge,

2004), 1–2, 65–98, on the military revolution in the Eurasian steppes and the Near East.

3. Adrienne Edgar, "Everyday Life among the Turkmen Nomads," in Jeff Sahadeo and Russell Zanca, eds., *Everyday Life in Central Asia Past and Present* (Bloomington; Indiana University Press, 2007), 38–44.

4. Owen Lattimore, *The Inner Asian Frontiers of China* (The American Geographical Society, 1940; repr., Hong Kong: Oxford University Press, 1988), 522.

5. Anthony, *The Horse*, 460.

6. Lien-Sheng Yang, "Historical Notes on the Chinese World Order" in John K. Fairbank (ed.), *The Chinese World Order* (Cambridge, MA.: Harvard University Press, 1970), 33. On Byzantine strategy, see Edward N. Luttwak, *The Grand Strategy of the Byzantine Empire* (Cambridge, MA.-London: The Belknap Press of Harvard University, 2009), 415–418.

7. See the remarkable quantity of goods studied by E. H. Schaefer, *The Golden Peaches of Samarkand: A Study of T'ang Exotics* (Berkeley: University of California Press, 1963; repr. 1985).

8. Hugh Pope, *Sons of the Conquerors. The Rise of the Turkic World* (New York: Overlook Duckworth, 2005), 316.

9. Colin Thubrun, *Shadow of the Silk Road* (New York: Harper Collins, 2007), 102.

10. Quintus Curtius, *History of Alexander*, trans. and ed. John C. Rolfe (Cambridge, MA: Harvard University Press, 1936; repr., 1985), 162–165.

11. Mahmûd al-Kâŝɣarî, *The Compendium of Turkic Dialects: Dîwân Luɣat at-Turk*, vol. 1, trans. and ed. Robert Dankoff in collaboration with James Kelly (Cambridge, MA: Harvard University Press, 1982–1985), 273. "*Tatsïz türk bolmas, bashsïz börk bolmas.*"

12. Denis Sinor, "Samoyed and Ugric Elements in Old Turkic," *Harvard Ukrainian Studies* 3–4 (1979–1980), 768–773, and "The Origin of Turkic *Balïq* 'Town'," *Central Asiatic Journal* 25 (1981), 95–102. Sinor has suggested that this word comes from the Ugric languages. There are a number of Ugric loan words in Turkic, although why the Turks would have borrowed this term from the hunting-gathering Ugric peoples is unclear.

CHAPTER 2

1. Elena E. Kuzmina, *The Prehistory of the Silk Road*, ed. Victor Mair (Philadelphia: University of Pennsylvania Press, 2008), 88–98.

2. Vera S. Rastorgueva and Dzhoi I. Edel'man, *Etimologicheskii slovar' iranskikh iazykov,* (Moscow: Vostochnaia Literatura, 2000-ongoing), 1: 222.

3. The subject remains hotly debated. See Edwin F. Bryant and Laurie L. Patton, eds., *The Indo-Aryan Controversy: Evidence and Inference in Indian History* (New York: Routledge, 2005) and Thomas R. Trautmann, ed., *The Aryan Debate* (New Delhi: Oxford University Press, 2005).

4. See A. Shapur Shahbazi, "The History of the Idea of Iran" in Vesta Sarkhosh Curtis and Sarah Stewart, eds., *Birth of the Persian Empire: The Idea of Iran*, vol. 1 (London: I. B. Tauris, 2005), 100–111.

5. Michael Witzel, *Linguistic Evidence for Cultural Exchange in Prehistoric Western Central Asia* in *Sino-Platonic Papers* 129 (December 2003): 13.

6. Herodotus, *The History*, trans. David Grene (Chicago: University of Chicago Press, 1987), 289.

7. Strabo, *The Geography of Strabo*, vol. 5, trans. H. L. Jones (Cambridge, Mass. Harvard University Press, 1944), 264–269.

8. Sima Qian, *Records of the Grand Historian: Han Dynasty*, vol. 2, trans. Burton Watson, 2nd rev. ed. (Hong Kong: Columbia University Press, 1993), 245.

9. Herodotus, *The History*, trans. Grene, 129–130.

10. See Justin J. Rudelson, *Oasis Identities* (New York: Columbia University Press, 1997), 66–68.

11. Frank L. Holt, *Into the Land of Bones: Alexander the Great in Afghanistan* (Berkeley: University of California Press, 2005), 86.

12. Nicola Di Cosmo, *Ancient China and its Enemies: The Rise of Nomadic Power in East Asian History* (Cambridge: Cambridge University Press, 2002), 186–188.

13. Sima Qian, trans. Watson, 129, 143.

14. Sima Qian, trans. Watson, 130, 134.

15. Sima Qian, trans. Watson, 143–144, notes the fondness of the Xiongnu for Chinese silk and foodstuffs, particularly grains, and their insistence that they be given "the right measure and quality."

16. Sima Qian, trans. Watson, 140–141.

17. Sima Qian, trans. Watson, 143.

18. Sima Qian, trans. Watson, 146.

19. Étienne de la Vaissière, *Sogdian Traders: A History*, trans. James Ward (Leiden: Brill, 2005), 28–32.

20. David Christian, "Silk Roads or Steppe Roads? The Silk Roads in World History," *Journal of World History* 11, no. 1 (2000): 1–26.

21. Thomas J. Barfield, *The Perilous Frontier: Nomadic Empires and China* (Oxford: Blackwell, 1989), 36.

22. Juha Janhunen, *Manchuria: An Ethnic History* (Helsinki: The Finno-Ugrian Society, 1996), 187.

23. For the most recent arguments in favor of this connection, see M Érdy, "Hun and Xiong-nu Type Cauldron Finds Throughout Eurasia" *Eurasian Studies Yearbook* 67 (1995), 5–94; D.C. Wright, "The Hsiung-nu–Hun Equation revisited" *Eurasian Studies Yearbook* 69 (1997), 77–112; E. Pulleyblank, "Tribal Confederations of Uncertain Identity. Hsiung-nu" in H.R. Roemer (ed.), *History of the Turkic Peoples in the Pre-Islamic Period. Philologiae et Historiae Turcicae Fundmenta*, I (= *Philologiae Turcicae Fundmenta*, III) (Berlin: Klaus Schwarz, 2000), 60; Étienne de la Vaissière, "Huns et Xiongnu," *Central Asiatic Journal* 49, no. 1 (2005): 3–26.

CHAPTER 3

1. They appear to have spoken a Mongolic language, see Alexander Vovin, "Once Again on the Tabgač Language" *Mongolia Studies* 29 (2007): 191–206.

2. Károly Czeglédy, "From East to West: The Age of Nomadic Migrations in Eurasia," *Archivum Eurasiae Medii Aevi* 3 (1983), pp. 67–106; Étienne de la Vaissière, "Is There Any Nationality of the Hephthalites?" *Bulletin of the Asia Institute* 17 (2003): 119–132.

3. R. C. Blockley, ed. and trans., *The Fragmentary Classicising Historians of the Later Roman Empire: Eunapius, Olympiodorus, Priscus and Malchus*, vol. 2 (Liverpool: Francis Cairns, 1981, 1983), 344–345.

4. *Türk* is used to denote the specific Turkic people bearing this name. *Turk* and *Turkic* are generic terms encompassing all the peoples speaking a Turkic language.

5. S. G. Klyashtornyi, "The Royal Clan of the Türks and the Problem of Early Turkic-Iranian Contacts," *Acta Orientalia Academiae Scientiarum Hungaricae* 47 no. 3 (1994): 445–448.

6. Liu Mau-tsai, *Die chinesischen Nachrichten zur Geschichte der Ost-Türken (T'u-küe)*, vol. 1 (Wiesbaden: Otto Harrassowitz, 1958): 5–6, 40–41.

7. Christopher I. Beckwith, *Empires of the Silk Road* (Princeton: Princeton University Press, 2009): 4, 6, 8–10.

8. See *The History of Theophylact Simocatta*, trans. Michael Whitby and Mary Whitby (Oxford: Clarendon Press, 1986): 188–190. Theophylact accuses the "European Avars" of having falsely adopted this famous name.

9. Liu, *Die chinesischen Nachrichten*, vol. 1, 87.

10. *The History of Menander the Guardsman*, ed. and trans. R. C. Blockley (Liverpool: Francis Cairns, 1985), 44–47.

11. *Menander*, ed. and trans. Blockley, 111–127, 173–175.

12. Liu Mau-tsai, *Die chinesischen Nachrichten*, vol. 1, 13.

13. *The Life of Hiuen Tsang By the Shaman Hwui Li*. With an introduction containing an account of the works of I-tsing, by Samuel Beal, Trubner's Oriental Series (London: K. Paul, Trench, Trubner, 1911), 42.

14. Ibid.

15. *Si-Yu-Ki. Buddhist Records of the Western World*, vol. 1, trans. Samuel Beal (London: Kegan Paul, Trench, Trübner, 1900) 28.

16. Yihong Pan, *Son of Heaven and Heavenly Qaghan: Sui-Tang China and its Neighbors* (Bellingham, Washington, 1997) 179–182, 191.

17. Christopher I. Beckwith, *The Tibetan Empire in Central Asia* (Princeton: Princeton University Press, 1987) 28–64.

18. Talât Tekin, *Orhon Yazıtları. Kül Tigin, Bilge Kagan, Tunyukuk* (Istanbul: Yıldız, 2003) 82.

19. Ibid.

20. Talât Tekin, *Orhon Yazıtları* (Ankara: Türk Dil Kurumu, 2006). See pp. 19–42 for the Kül Tegin inscription and pp. 44–70 for the Bilge Qaghan inscription.

21. The Shine Usu inscription in Takao Moriyasu and Ayudai Ochir, eds., *Provisional Report of Researches on Historical Sites and Inscriptions in Mongolia from 1996 to 1998* (Osaka: The Society of Central Asian Studies, 1999) 183.

22. Colin Mackerras, *The Uighur Empire According to the T'ang Dynastic Histories* (Canberra: Australian National University Press, 1972) 122.

23. Vladimir F. Minorsky, "Tamîm ibn Baḥr's Journey to the Uyghurs," *Bulletin of the School of Oriental and African Studies* 12 no. 2 (1948): 275–305.

24. Judith G. Kolbas, "Khukh Ordung, a Uighur Palace Complex of the Seventh Century," *Journal of the Royal Asiatic Society* 15 no. 3 (November 2005): 303–327.

25. I. V. Kormushin, *Tiurkskie eniseiskie epitafii. Teksty i issledovaniia* (Moscow: Nauka, 1997): 121–122.

26. Ibn al-Faqîh, *Kitâb al-Buldân*, ed. M. J. de Goeje (Leiden: Brill, 1885) 329.

CHAPTER 4

1. Al-Muqadassî, Ahsan at-Taqâsîm fî Ma'rîfat al-Aqâlîm. Descriptio imperii moslemici auctore Schamso'd-dîn Abdollâh Mohammed ibn Ahmed ibn abî

Bekr al-Bannâ al-Basschârî al-Mokaddesî, ed. M. J. de Goeje (Leiden: Brill, 1877; 2nd ed. 1906), 324–325.

2. Étienne De la Vaissière, *Sogdian Traders. A History*, trans. James Ward (Leiden: Brill, 2005), 148–152.

3. For samples of these letters, see W. B. Henning, "The Date of the Sogdian Ancient Letters," *Bulletin of the School of Oriental and African Studies* 12 no. 3–4 (1948), 601–616; Nicholas Sims-Williams, "Towards a New Edition of the Sogdian Ancient Letters: Ancient Letter I" in *Les Sogdiens en Chine*, ed. Étienne de la Vaissière and Eric Trombert (Paris: École Française d'Extrême Orient, 2005), 181–193; and Nicholas Sims-Williams, "The Sogdian Ancient Letters," http://depts.washington.edu/silkroad/texts/sogdlet.html.

4. *Si-Yu-Ki: Buddhist Records of the Western World*, vol. 2, trans. Samuel Beal (London: Kegan Paul, Trench, Trübner, 1900), 43–44.

5. *Si-Yu-Ki*, vol. 2, trans. Beal, 318–319; Hans Wilhelm Haussig, *Die Geschichte Zentrasiens und der Seidenstrasse in vorislamischer Zeit* (Darmstadt: Wissenschaftliche Buchgesellschaft, 1983), 68.

6. *Si-Yu-Ki*. vol. 2, trans. Beal, 309, 315–316.

7. Sir Aurel Stein, *On Central Asian Tracks* (New York: Pantheon Books, 1964), 56.

8. Yutaka Yoshida, "On the Origin of the Sogdian Surname Zhaowu 昭武 and Related Problems," *Journal Asiatique* 291/1–2 (2003): 35–67.

9. Narshakhî, *The History of Bukhara*, trans. Richard N. Frye, (Cambridge, MA: The Mediaeval Academy of America, 1954), 9–10.

10. Narshakhî, trans. Frye, pp.30–31.

11. Étienne de la Vaissière, *Samarcande et Samarra. Élites d'Asie Centrale dans l'empire Abbaside* (Paris: Association pour l'avancement des études iraniennes, 2007), 69–70, 86.

12. Richard N. Frye, *Ancient Iran* (Munich: C. H. Beck, 1984), 351–352.

13. B. Marshak, *Legends, Tales, and Fables in the Art of Sogdiana* (New York: Bibliotheca Persica, 2002), 17, 65–67.

14. W. B. Henning, "Sogdian Tales," *Bulletin of the School of Oriental and African Studies* 11 no. 3 (1945): 485–487.

15. *The Life of Hiuen Tsang By the Shaman Hwui Li*. With an introduction containing an account of the works of I-tsing, by Samuel Beal, Trubner's Oriental Series (London: K. Paul, Trench, Trubner, 1911), 45.

16. Edouard Chavannes, *Documents sur les Tou-kiue (Turcs) Occidentaux* (Paris: Librairie d'Amérique et d'Orient, 1941; repr. Taipei: Ch'eng Wen Publishing, 1969), 135.

17. Chavannes, *Documents*, 33 n.5; B. G. Gafurov, *Tadzhiki* (Moscow: Nauka, 1972), 284.

18. Al-Bîrûnî, *Al-Athâr al-Baqiyya 'an Qurûn al-Khâliyya, Chronologie orietalischer Völker*, ed. C. Eduard Sachau (Leipzig: Otto Harrassowitz, 1929), 234–235.

19. Chavannes, *Documents*, 139.

20. Chavannes, *Documents*, 133 n.5.

21. Chavannes, *Documents*, 148.

22. Frantz Grenet, Étienne de la Vaissière, "The Last Days of Panjikent," *Silk Road Art and Archaeology* 8 (2002): 167–171; and *Sogdiiskie dokumenty s gory Mug*, ed. and trans. V. A. Livshits (Moscow: Vostochnaia Literatura, 1962), 2: 78–79.

23. Al-Tabarî, *The History of al-Tabarî: The End of Expansion,* vol. 25, ed. Ehsan Yar-Shater, trans. Khalid Yahya Blankenship (Albany: State University of New York Press, 1989), 143–149.

24. Jonathan Bloom, *Paper Before Print: The History and Impact of Paper on the Islamic World* (New Haven: Yale University Press, 2001), 38–40, 42–45.

25. Al-Bîrûnî, *Al-Athâr,* ed. Eduard Sachau, 36, 48.

CHAPTER 5

1. Rashîd al-Dîn, *Die Geschichte der Oğuzen des Rašîd ad-Dîn,* ed. and trans. Karl Jahn (Vienna: Hermann Böhlaus Nachf., 1969), 23–25.

2. *Hudûd al-'Âlam: The Regions of the World,* 2nd ed., trans. Vladimir Minorsky, ed. C. E. Bosworth, E. J. W. Gibb Memorial Series, new series, 11 (London: Luzac, 1970), 96–97.

3. Al-Câhiz [Al-Jâhiz:], *Hilâfet Ordusunun Menkıbeleri ve Türkler'in Fazîletleri,* ed. Turkish trans. Ramazan Şeşen (Ankara: Türk Kültürünü Araştırma Enstitüsü, 1967), 68.

4. Analyzed in Omeljan Pritsak, *Die bulgarischen Fürstenliste und die Sprache der Protobulgaren* (Wiesbaden: Otto Harrassowitz, 1955).

5. Abu Bakr Muhammad ibn Ja'far Narshakhî, *The History of Bukhara,* trans. Richard N. Frye, (Cambridge, MA: The Mediaeval Academy of America, 1954), 34.

6. Jürgen Paul, "Islamizing Sûfis in Pre-Mongol Central Asia," in E. de la Vaissière, ed., *Islamisation de l'Asie centrale,* Studia Iranica 39 (Paris: Association pour l'avancement des études iraniennes, 2008): 297–317. Contrary to earlier scholarship, Paul argues that Sûfîs did not play a significant role in Islamizing the Central Asian Turks until the Mongol era.

7. Ibn al-Athîr, *Al-Kâmil fî'l-Ta'rîkh: Chronicon quod perfectissimum inscribitur,* ed. C. J. Tornberg (Leiden, 1851–76; repr. Beirut, 1965–66 with different pagination), 9: 520.

8. W. Barthold, *Turkestan Down to the Mongol Invasion,* trans. T. Minorsky, ed. C. E. Bosworth (London, 1968), 312.

9. Al-Utbi, *The Kitab i Yamini. Historical Memoirs of the Amír Sabaktagin, and the Sultán Mahmúd of Ghazna,* trans. Rev. James Reynolds (London: Oriental Translation Fund of Great Britain and Ireland, 1858), 140.

10. C. E. Bosworth, *The Ghaznavids: Their Empire in Afghanistan and Eastern Iran 994: 1040* (Edinburgh: Edinburgh University Press, 1963), 115–116.

11. Yûsuf Khâss Hâjib, *Wisdom of Royal Glory (Kutadgu Bilig): A Turko-Islamic Mirror for Princes,* trans. Robert Dankoff (Chicago: University of Chicago Press, 1983), 49.

12. Ibid., 48.

13. Ibid., 48–49.

14. Mahmûd al-Kâšyarî, *The Compendium of Turkic Dialects. Dîwân Luγāt at-Turk,* ed. and trans. Robert Dankoff in collaboration with James Kelly (Cambridge, MA; Harvard University Press, 1982–1985), 1: 109, 364; 2: 184–185.

CHAPTER 6

1. On the rise of the Qara Khitai, see Michal Biran, *The Empire of the Qara Khitai in Eurasian History* (Cambridge: Cambridge University Press, 2005), 19–47.

2. 'Ata-Malik Juvainî, *The History of the World-Conqueror*, trans. John A. Boyle (Cambridge, MA,: Harvard University Press, 1958), 1: 21–22.

3. *The Secret History of the Mongols,* trans. Igor de Rachewiltz (Leiden-Boston: Brill, 2004), 1: 10, 287.

4. Rashîd ad-Dîn, *Jâmi' at-Tavârîkh*, ed. Muhammad Rowshan and Mustafâ Mûsavî (Tehran: Nashr-i Alburz, 1373/1994), 1: 251–252.

5. *The Secret History*, trans. de Rachewiltz, 1: 13.

6. *The Secret History*, trans. de Rachewiltz, 1: 4.

7. *The Secret History*, trans. de Rachewiltz, 1: 19–20.

8. Rashîd ad-Dîn, *Jâmi' at-Tavârîkh*, ed. Rowshan and Mûsavî, 1: 361–4.

9. Juvainî, *History*, trans. Boyle, 1:107, 122.

10. Rashîd al-Dîn, *The Successors of Genghis Khan*, trans. John A. Boyle (New York: Columbia University Press, 1971), 17–18.

11. Peter Jackson, "From *Ulus* to Khanate" in Reuven Amitai-Preiss and David Morgan, eds., *The Mongol Empire and its Legacy* (Leiden: Brill, 1999), 12–38.

12. S. A. M. Adshead, *Central Asia in World History* (New York: St. Martin's Press, 1993), 61.

13. Kirakos Gandzaketsi, *Istoriia Armenii*, trans. L. A. Khanlarian (Moscow: Nauka, 1976), 156.

14. Minhâj al-Dîn al-Juzjânî, *Tabaqât-i Nâsirî*, ed. 'Abd al-Hayy Habîbî (Tehran: Dunyâ-yi Kitâb, 1363/1984), 2: 197–198.

15. Reuven Amitai-Preiss, *Mongols and Mamluks: The Mamluk—Ilkhânid War, 1260–1281* (Cambridge: Cambridge University Press, 1995), 1.

16. See Marco Polo, *The Travels of Marco Polo: The Complete Yule-Cordier Edition* (New York: Dover, 1993), 2: 463–65, where she is called by her Turkic name "Aijaruc" (*Ay Yaruq,* Bright Moon). Michal Biran, *Qaidu and the Rise of the Independent Mongol State in Central Asia* (Richmond, UK: Curzon, 1997), 1–2, 19–67.

17. Peter Jackson, "The Mongols and the Faith of the Conquered" in Reuven Amitai and Michal Biran, eds., *Mongols, Turks, and Others: Eurasian Nomads and the Sedentary World* (Leiden: Brill, 2005), 245–278.

18. Rashid al-Din, *Successors*, trans. Boyle, 37.

19. Thomas T. Allsen, *Culture and Conquest in Mongol Eurasia* (Cambridge: Cambridge University Press, 2001), 63–89, 177–179.

20. Rashîd ad-Dîn, *Jâmi' at-Tavârîkh*, ed. Rowshan and Mûsavî, 2: 1137–1138.

21. Paul D. Buell, "Mongol Empire and Turkicization: The Evidence of Food and Foodways" in Reuven Amitai-Preiss and David O. Morgan, eds., *The Mongol Empire and its Legacy* (Leiden: Brill, 1999), 200–223.

22. Peter B. Golden, ed., *The King's Dictionary: The Rasûld Hexaglot* (Leiden-Boston-Köln, 2000), 112, 227.

23. William of Rubruck, *The Mission of Friar William of Rubruck*, trans. Peter Jackson, ed. Peter Jackson and David Morgan, Hakluyt Society, second series, vol. 173 (London: Hakluyt Society, 1990), esp. 76–77, 183, 209–210.

24. Thomas T. Allsen, "Command Performances: Entertainers in the Mongolian Empire," *Russian Histoire-Histoire Russe*, 28, no. 1–4 (Winter 2001): 41–45.

25. Ibid., 38–41.

26. Jerry H. Bentley, "Cross-Cultural Interaction and Periodization in World History," *American Historical Review,* 101, no. 3 (June 1996): 766–767.

1. Al-'Umarî, *Das mongolische Weltreich. Al-'Umarî's Darstellung der mongolis-chen Reiche in seinem Werk Masâlik al-abṣâr fî mamalik al-amṣâr*, ed. with German paraphrase by Klaus Lech, *Asiatische Forschungen*, Bd. 22 (Wiesbaden: Harrassowitz, 1968), Arabic text, p. 73.

2. Jean-Paul Roux, *La religion des Turcs et des Mongols* (Paris: Payot, 1984), 137–141.

3. Devin DeWeese, *Islamization and Native Religion in the Golden Horde* (University Park, PA: Penn State Press, 1994), 541–543.

4. David M. Abramson and Elyor E. Karimov, "Sacred Sites, Profane Ideologies: Religious Pilgrimage and the Uzbek State" in Jeff Sahadeo and Russell Zanca, eds., *Everyday Life in Central Asia Past and Present* (Bloomington: Indiana University Press, 2007),–338.

5. Toktobiubiu Dzh. Baialieva, *Doislamskie verovaniia i ikh perezhitki u kirgizov* (Frunze, Kyrgyz SSR: Ilim, 1972), 140–142, 149–151.

6. Don Ruiz Gonzales de Clavijo, *Embassy to Tamerlane 1403–1406*, trans. Guy Le Strange (London: Routledge, 1928, repr. Frankfurt am-Main, 1994), pp. 137, 212.

7. Clavijo, *Embassy to Tamerlane*, trans. Le Strange, 210.

8. Ibid., 210–211.

9. Ibid., 286.

10. The oft-repeated story of the *Kök Tash*'s association with Temür appears to be an eighteenth-century creation, fully accepted by nineteenth-century visitors to the site. None of the contemporary accounts note it, see Ron Sela, "The 'Heavenly Stone' (Kök Tash) of Samarqand: A Rebels' Narrative Transformed" *Journal of the Royal Asiatic Society* 17/1 (2007), 21–32.

11. Colin Thubron, *Shadow of the Silk Road* (New York: Harper Collins, 2007), 199.

12. Tilman Nagel, *Timur der Eroberer und die islamische Welt des späten Mittelalters* (Munich: Verlag C.H. Beck, 1993), 337–339.

13. Filiz Çağman, "Glimpses into the Fourteenth-Century Turkic World of Central Asia: The Paintings of Muhammad Siyah Qalam" in David J. Roxburgh, ed., *Turks: A Journey of a Thousand Years, 600–1600* (London: Royal Academy of Arts, 2005), 148–190. Examples of Timurid art can be found in David J. Roxburgh, "The Timurid and Turkmen Dynasties of Iran, Afghanistan and Central Asia c. 1370–1506" in Roxburgh ed., *Turks*, 192–260.

14. See Allen J. Frank, *Islamic Historiography and 'Bulghar' Identity among the Tatars and Bashkirs of Russia* (Leiden: Brill, 1998).

15. S. K. Ibragimov et al., eds., *Materialy po istorii kazakhskikh khanstv XV-XVIII vekov* (Alma-Ata: Nauka, 1969), 169.

16. *Qazaq* was later borrowed into Russian (*kazak*) and Ukrainian (*kozak*) to denote a free, largely Slavic population on the frontiers of the steppe: the Cossacks.

17. Mirza Muhammad Haidar Dughlat, *A History of the Moghuls of Central Asia being the Tarikh-i Rashidi*, ed. N. Elias, trans. E. Dennison Ross (London, 1895; repr. London: Curzon Press, 1972), 82.

18. Ibid., 14–15, 58.

19. Johan Elverskog, ed. and trans., *The Jewel Translucent Sūtra. Altan Khan and the Mongols in the Sixteenth Century* (Leiden: Brill, 2003), 8–9, 48–52, 71.

20. Kenneth Chase, *Firearms: A Global History to 1700* (Cambridge: Cambridge University Press, 2003), 52–53, 55, 61; Peter C. Perdue, *China Marches West The Qing Conquest of Central Eurasia* (Cambridge, MA: The Belknap Press of Harvard University Press, 2005), 58–59.

CHAPTER 8

1. Chase, *Firearms*, 124, 203.

2. Dughlat, *Tarikh-i Rashîdî*, ed. Elias, trans. Ross, 272–273.

3. *The Baburnama: Memoirs of Babur, Prince and Emperor*, ed. and trans. Wheeler M. Thackston (New York: Oxford University Press, 1996), 256.

4. *Baburnama*, ed. and trans. Thackston, 46.

5. Michael Khodarkovsky, *Russia's Steppe Frontier: The Making of a Colonial Empire 1500–1800* (Bloomington: University of Indiana Press, 2002), 21–22.

6. Vadim V. Trepavlov, *Istoriia nogaiskoi ordy* [History of the Noghai Horde] (Moscow: Vostochnaia Literatura, 2001), 372–375.

7. She is depicted as a blood-drinking old woman dressed in red. See Ruth I. Meserve, "The Red Witch" in *The Role of Women in the Altaic World*. Permanent International Altaistic Conference, 44th Meeting, Walberberg, 26–31 August 2001, ed. Veronika Veit, Asiatische Forschungen, Bd. 152 (Wiesbaden: Harrassowitz, 2007), 131–141.

8. From Chinese *Huang Taizi*, "Respected Son," Mark C. Elliot, *The Manchu Way* (Stanford, CA: Stanford University Press, 2001), 63, 396–397n71.

9. Giovanni Stary, "The Meaning of the Word 'Manchu.' A New Solution to an Old Problem," *Central Asiatic Journal* 34, no.1–2 (1990), 109–119. Stary derives it from Manchu *man*, "strong, powerful, great" combined with the suffix *–ju*, which expresses a wished-for realization: "May you be strong, powerful, great."

10. For the text of the treaty and facsimiles of the Russian and Manchu texts, see Basil Dmytryshyn et al. eds. and trans., *Russia's Conquest of Siberia: A Documentary Record 1558–1700* (Portland, OR: Western Imprints, The Press of the Oregon Historical Society, 1985), 497–501.

11. Fred. W. Bergholz, *The Partition of the Steppe:. The Struggle of the Russians, Manchus and the Zunghar Mongols for Empire in Central Asia, 1619–1758* (New York: Peter Lang, 1993), 270–277, 335–340; Perdue, *China Marches West*, 161–173.

12. Arthur Waldron, *The Great Wall of China: From History to Myth* (Cambridge: Cambridge University Press, 1990), 3–4, 122–164.

13. Lubsan Danzan (Lubsangdanjin), *Altan Tobchi* [The Golden Summary], trans. N. P. Shastina (Moscow: Nauka, 1973), 290; Johan Elverskog, ed. and trans. *The Jewel Translucent Sūtra* (Leiden: Brill, 2003), 129–130.

14. Tsongkhapa was considered the first Dalai Lama. The interview was conducted through interpreters, and some misunderstandings of terminology and protocol may have occurred.

15. Lubsan Danzan, *Altan Tobchi*, 291–292.

16. She had been one of the wives of Altan Khan's father. In keeping with old steppe practice, the heir often married his father's wife (other than one's mother) or wives and those of deceased brothers as well See C. R. Bawden, *The Modern History of Mongolia* (New York: Frederick Praeger, 1968), 28–29.

17. Bawden, *The Modern History of Mongolia*, 27–28, citing the account of Xiao Daheng, written in 1594, a generation after the conversion.

18. Elverskog, ed. and trans., *The Jewel Translucent Sūtra*, 35–40.

19. The various views on this much-debated subject are found in Scott C. Levi, *Indian and Central Asia: Commerce and Culture, 1500–1800* (New Delhi: Oxford University Press, 2007).

20. A. I. Levshin, *Opisanie kirgiz-kazatskikh ili kirgiz-kaisatskikh ord i stepei* (St. Petersburg, 1832, repr. Almaty: Sanat, 1996), 313.

21. For the debate on the nature of Kazakh religious practices, see Bruce G. Privratsky, *Muslim Turkistan* (Richmond, Surrey: Curzon, 2001), 7–29 and the cautionary remarks of Devin De Weese, *Islamization and Native Religion in the Golden Horde* (University Park, PA: The Pennsylvania State Press 1994), 65-6, with regard to the alleged "superficiality" of Kyrgyz Islam.

22. Questions regarding the long-established popular etymology of this name are raised by Christopher I. Beckwith, "A Note on the Name and Identity of the Junghars," *Mongolian Studies* 29 (2007): 41–45.

23. Valentin A. Riasanovsky, *The Fundamental Principles of Mongol Law* (Tientsin, 1937: repr. in Indiana University Uralic and Altaic Series, vol. 43, The Hague: Mouton, 1965), 92–100.

24. Peter C. Perdue, *China Marches West. The Qing Conquest of Central Eurasia* (Cambridge, MA: The Belknap Press of Harvard University Press), 140.

25. Perdue, *China Marches West*, 304–306; Millward, *Eurasian Crossroads*, 89–90.

26. From the *Da Qing Shengzu Ren Huangdi Shilu* [Decree of Emperor Kangxi of August 4, 1690] in B. P. Gurevich and G. F. Kim, eds., *Mezhdunarodnye otnosheniia v Tsentral'noi Azii. XVII-XVIII vv. Dokumenty i materialy* (Moscow: Nauka, 1989), 1:195–196.

27. Dughlat, *Tarikh-i Rashîdî*, ed. Elias, trans. Ross, 125, 148.

28. Buri A. Akhmedov, ed. and trans., *Makhmud ibn Vali, More tain otnositel'no doblestei blagorodnykh* [a translation of Mahmûd ibn Walî, *Bahr al-Asrâr fî Manâqib al-Akhyâr*] (Tashkent: Fan, 1977), 41.

CHAPTER 9

1. Captain John Moubray Trotter, compiler, "Central Asia", Section II, Part IV. *A Contribution towards the Better Knowledge of the Topography, Ethnography, Resources and History of the Khanat of Bokhara* (Calcutta: Foreign Department Press, 1873), 3–6.

2. Lieutenant Alexander Burnes, *Travels into Bukhara* (London: John Murray, 1834), 1: 267–270.

3. Frederick G. Burnaby, *A Ride To Khiva* (London: Cassell Petter & Galpin, 1876, repr. Oxford: Oxford University Press, 1997), 307, 309–310.

4. Eugene Schuyler, *Turkestan: Notes of a Journey in Russian Turkestan, Khokand, Bukhara and Kuldja* (London: Sampson Low, Marston Searle, and Rivington, 1876), 2: 6, 11.

5. Schuler, *Turkestan*, 1: 162.

6. Burnes, *Travels*, 1: 252.

7. Ibid., 1: 276.

8. Robert D. Crews, *For Prophet and Tsar: Islam and Empire in Russia and Central Asia* (Cambridge, MA: Harvard University Press, 2006), 38.

9. Mîrzâ 'Abdal 'Azîm Sâmî, *Ta'rîkh-i Salâtîn-i Manġitîya (Istoriia mangytskikh gosudarei)*, ed. and trans. L. M. Epifanova (Moscow: Vostochnaia Literatura, 1962), 119 (109b); and Jo-Ann Gross, "Historical Memory, Cultural Identity,

of Bukhara" in Daniel R. Brower and Edward J. Lazzarini, eds., *Russia's Orient: Imperial Borderlands and Peoples, 1700–1917* (Bloomington: Indiana University Press, 1997), 216.

10. Robert D. Crews, "Empire and the Confessional State: Islam and Religious Politics in Nineteenth-century Russia," *The American Historical Review* 108, no.1 (February 2003), 50–52.

11. Chokan Ch. Valikhanov, "Ocherki Dzhungarii," in his *Sobranie Sochinenii,* 5 vols. (Alma-Ata: Kazakhstaia Sovetskaia Entsiklopediia, 1984–1985) 3:327.

12. M.Kh. Abuseitova et al., *Istoriia Kazakhstana i Tsentral'noi Azii* (Almaty: Bilim, 2001), 409.

13. Edward Allworth, ed., *Central Asia:. 130 Years of Russian Dominance, A Historical Overview,* 3rd. ed. (Durham: University of North Carolina Press, 1994), 98.

14. Jacob Landau and Barbara Kellner-Heinkele, *Politics of Language in the Ex-Soviet Muslim States* (Ann Arbor: University of Michigan Press, 2001), 7.

15. SergeiAbashin, *Natsionalizmy v Srednei Azii. V poiskakh identichnosti* (Sankt-Peterburg: Aleteiia, 2007), 186–189.

16. Peter Fincke, "Competing Ideologies of Statehood and Governance in Central Asia: Turkic Dynasties in Transoxania and their Legacy" in David Sneath, ed., *States of Mind: Power, Place, and the Subject in Inner Asia,* Center for East Asian Studies, Western Washington University for Mongolia and Inner Asia Studies Unit, University of Cambridge (Bellingham: Western Washington University, 2006), 111–112.

17. Pope, *Sons of the Conquerors,* 234–239.

18. Landau and Kellner-Heinkele, *Politics,* 124–147.

19. Pope, *Sons of the Conquerors,* 293.

20. *New York Times,* August 7, 2009, A4.

Further Reading

REFERENCE WORKS

Abazov, Rafis. *Palgrave Concise Historical Atlas of Central Asia*. New York: Palgrave Macmillan, 2008.

Atwood, Christopher P. *Encyclopedia of Mongolia and the Mongol Empire*. New York: Facts on File, 2004.

Bosworth, Clifford Edmund. *The New Islamic Dynasties*. New York: Columbia University Press, 1996.

Bregel, Yuri. *An Historical Atlas of Central Asia*. Leiden: Brill, 2003.

GENERAL STUDIES

Adshead, S. A. M. *Central Asia in World History*. New York: St. Martin's Press, 1993.

André, Paul. *The Art of Central Asia*. London: Parkstone Press, 1996.

Barfield, Thomas. *Perilous Frontiers: Nomadic Empires and China*. Oxford: Blackwell, 1987.

Basilov, V. N. *Nomads of Eurasia*. Translated by M. F. Zirin. Seattle, WA: University of Washington Press, 1989.

Beckwith, Christopher I. *Empires of the Silk Road*. Princeton: Princeton University Press, 2009.

Çağatay, Ergun, and Doğan Kuban, eds. *The Turkic Speaking Peoples: 2000 Years of Art and Culture from Inner Asia to the Balkans*. Munich: Prestel, 2006.

Canfield, Robert L., ed. *Turko-Persia in Historical Perspective*. Cambridge: Cambridge University Press, 1991.

Christian, David. *A History of Russia, Central Asia and Mongolia*. Vol. 1, *Inner Eurasia from Prehistory to the Mongol Empire*. Oxford: Blackwell, 1998.

Di Cosmo, Nicola, Allen J. Frank, and Peter B. Golden, eds. *The Cambridge History of Inner Asia: The Chinggisid Age*. Cambridge: Cambridge University Press, 2009.

Findley, Carter V. *The Turks in World History*. New York: Oxford University Press, 2004.

Foltz, Richard C. *Religions of the Silk Road*. New York: St. Martin's Press, 1999.

Grousset, René. *The Empire of the Steppes*. Translated by Naomi Walford. New Brunswick: Rutgers University Press, 1970.

Hambly, Gavin, ed., *Central Asia*. New York: Delacorte Press, 1969.

Jagchid, Sechin, and Paul Hyer. *Mongolia's Culture and Society*. Boulder, CO: Westview Press, 1979.

Khazanov, Anatoly M. *Nomads and the Outside World*. Cambridge: Cambridge University Press, 1984.

Lattimore, Owen. *The Inner Asian Frontiers of China*. American Geographical Society, 1940. Reprint, Hong Kong: Oxford University Press, 1988.

Liu, Xinru. *The Silk Road in World History*. New York: Oxford University Press, 2010.

Millward, James A. *Eurasian Crossroads: A History of Xinjiang*. New York: Columbia University Press, 2007.

Roxburgh, David J., ed. *Turks: A Journey of a Thousand Years, 600–1600*. London: Royal Academy of Arts, 2005.

Sinor, Denis, ed., *The Cambridge History of Early Inner Asia*. Cambridge: Cambridge University Press, 1990.

Soucek, Svat. *A History of Inner Asia*. Cambridge: Cambridge University Press, 2000.

ANCIENT

Anthony, David W. *The Horse, the Wheel, and Language: How Bronze-Age Riders from the Eurasian Steppes Shaped the World*. Princeton: Princeton University Press, 2007.

Di Cosmo, Nicola. *Ancient China and its Enemies: The Rise of Nomadic Power in East Asian History*. Cambridge: Cambridge University Press, 2002.

Cribb, Joe, and Georgina Herrmann. *After Alexander: Central Asia Before Islam*. Oxford: Oxford University Press, 2007.

Kohl, Philip L. *The Making of Bronze Age Eurasia*. Cambridge: Cambridge University Press, 2007.

Mallory, J. P., and Victor Mair. *The Tarim Mummies*. London: Thames and Hudson, 2000.

MEDIEVAL

Allsen, Thomas T. *Culture and Conquest in Mongol Eurasia*. Cambridge: Cambridge University Press, 2001.

———. "The Rise of the Mongolian Empire and Mongolian Rule in North China." *The Cambridge History of China*. Vol. 6, *Alien Regimes and Border States, 907–1368*. Edited by Herbert Franke and Denis Twitchett. Cambridge: Cambridge University Press, 1994.

Anonymous. *The Secret History of the Mongols*. Translated by Igor de Rachewiltz. 2 vols. Leiden-Boston: Brill, 2004.

Barthold, W. [V. V. Bartol'd]. *Turkestan Down to the Mongol Invasion*. 3rd ed. Translated by T. Minorsky. Edited by C. E. Bosworth. London, 1968.

Beckwith, Christopher I. *The Tibetan Empire in Central Asia*. Princeton: Princeton University Press, 1993.

Biran, Michal. *The Empire of the Qara Khitai in Eurasian History*. Cambridge: Cambridge University Press, 2005.

Clavijo, Don Ruiz Gonzales de. *Embassy to Tamerlane 1403–1406*. Translated by Guy Le Strange. London: Routledge, 1928. Reprint, Frankfurt-am-Main, 1994.

Dawson, Christopher, ed. *Mission to Asia*. London: Sheed and Ward, 1980.

de la Vaissière, Étienne. *Sogdian Traders: A History*. Translated by James Ward. Leiden: Brill, 2005.

DeWeese, Devin. *Islamization and Native Religion in the Golden Horde*. University Park: Penn State Press, 1994.

Frye, Richard N. *The Heritage of Central Asia*. Princeton: Markus Wiener, 1996.

Hâjib, Yûsuf Khâss. *Wisdom of Royal Glory (Kutadgu Bilig): A Turko-Islamic Mirror for Princes*. Translated by Robert Dankoff. Chicago: University of Chicago Press, 1983.

Jackson, Peter. *The Mongols and the West, 1221–1410*. New York: Pearson Longman, 2005.

Juvainî, 'Ata-Malik. *The History of the World-Conqueror*. Translated by John A. Boyle. Cambridge, MA: Harvard University Press, 1958.

Mackerras, Colin. *The Uighur Empire According to the T'ang Dynastic Histories*. Canberra: Australian National University Press, 1972.

Manz, Beatrice F. *The Rise and Rule of Tamerlane*. Cambridge: Cambridge University Press, 1989.

Marshak, Boris. *Legends, Tales, and Fables in the Art of Sogdiana*. New York: Bibliotheca Persica Press, 2002.

Morgan, David. *The Mongols*. Oxford: Blackwell, 1986.

Narshakhî, Abu Bakr Muhammad ibn Ja'far. *The History of Bukhara*. Translated by Richard N. Frye. Cambridge, MA: The Mediaeval Academy of America, 1954.

Pan, Yihong. *Son of Heaven and Heavenly Qaghan: Sui-Tang China and its Neighbors*. Bellingham, WA: Western Washington University Press, 1997.

Polo, Marco. *The Travels of Marco Polo: The Complete Yule-Cordier Edition*. 2 vols. New York: Dover, 1993.

Rashîd al-Dîn, Fadlallâh. *The Successors of Genghis Khan*. Translated by John A. Boyle. New York: Columbia University Press, 1971.

Ratchnevsky, Paul. *Genghis Khan: His Life and Legacy*. Translated by Thomas N. Haining. Oxford: Blackwell, 1991.

Rubruck, William of. *The Mission of Friar William of Rubruck*. Translated by Peter Jackson. Edited by Peter Jackson and David Morgan. Hakluyt Society, second series, vol. 173. London: Hakluyt Society, 1990.

Wriggins, Sally Hovey. *Xuanzang: A Buddhist Pilgrim on the Silk Road*. Boulder, CO: Westview Press, 1996.

EARLY MODERN

Babur. *The Baburnama: Memoirs of Babur, Prince and Emperor*. Translated, edited, and annotated by Wheeler M. Thackston. New York: Oxford Universty Press, 1998.

Bergholz, Fred W. *The Partition of the Steppe: The Struggle of the Russians, Manchus, and the Zunghar Mongols for Empire in Central Asia, 1619–1758*. New York: Peter Lang, 1993.

Dughlat, Mirza Muhammad Haidar. *A History of the Moghuls of Central Asia being the Tarikh-i Rashidi*. Edited by N. Elias. Translated by E. Dennison Ross. London, 1895. Reprint, London: Curzon Press, 1972.

Perdue, Peter C. *China Marches West: The Qing Conquest of Central Eurasia*. Cambridge, MA: The Belknap Press of Harvard University Press, 2005.

MODERN

Allworth, Edwin. *Central Asia: 130 Years of Russian Dominance, A Historical Overview*. 3rd ed. Durham, NC: Duke University Press, 2002.

Bawden, Charles R. *The Modern History of Mongolia*. New York: Frederick Praeger, 1968.

Brower, Daniel R., and Edward J. Lazzarini, eds. *Russia's Orient. Imperial Borderlands and Peoples, 1700–1917*. Bloomington: Indiana University Press, 1997.

Crews, Robert D. *For Prophet and Tsar: Islam and Empire in Russia and Central Asia*. Cambridge, MA: Harvard University Press, 2006.

d'Encausse, Hélène Carrère. *Islam and the Russian Empire: Reform and Revolution in Central Asia*. Translated by Quintin Hoare. Berkeley: University of California Press, 1988.

Hiro, Dilip. *Inside Central Asia: A Political and Cultural History of Uzbekistan, Turkmenistan, Kazakhstan, Kyrgyz*. New York: Overlook Duckworth, 2009.

Khalid, Adeeb. *Islam after Communism: Religion and Politics in Central Asia*. Berkeley: University of California Press, 2007.

Khalid, Adeeb. *The Politics of Muslim Cultural Reform: Jadidism in Central Asia*. Berkeley: University of California Press, 1998.

Khodarkovsky, Michael. *Russia's Steppe Frontier: The Making of a Colonial Empire 1500–1800*. Bloomington, IN: University of Indiana Press, 2002.

Landau, Jacob, and Barbara Kellner-Heinkele. *Politics of Language in the Ex-Soviet Muslim States*. Ann Arbor, MI: University of Michigan Press, 2001.

Northrop, Douglas. *Veiled Empire: Gender and Power in Stalinist Central Asia*. Ithaca, NY: Cornell University Press, 2004.

Roy, Olivier. *The New Central Asia: The Creation of Nations*. New York: New York University Press, 2000.

Rudelson, Justin J. *Oasis Identities: Uyghur Nationalism Along China's Silk Road*. New York: Columbia University Press, 1997.

Sahadeo, Jeff, and Russell Zanca, eds. *Everyday Life in Central Asia Past and Present*. Bloomington: Indiana University Press, 2007.

Websites

Asia Society: Country Profiles
www.asiasociety.org/countries-history/country-profiles

This excellent reference website provides a clear and current overview and statistics about the countries of Asia, including Central Asia. Illustrated with maps and flags.

Buddhist Art and Trade Routes
www.asiasocietymuseum.com/buddhist_trade/index.html

The Asia Society hosts this website of images, maps, and articles about Buddhist art and the Silk Road.

Central Eurasia Project of the Open Society Institute
www.eurasianet.org/

This news website covers economic and civil topics in Central Asia. Articles are supplemented by interviews, slideshows, blogs, and videos.

Dunhuang Academy
www.dha.ac.cn/

This website provides photos and information on the history of selected grottos from the Mogao caves.

Heilbrunn Timeline of Art History
www.metmuseum.org/toah/

The Metropolitan Museum of Art provides timelines and articles on art from all over the world, divided into regions. The geographic section "Central and North Asia" is most relevant. The site includes essays devoted to Genghis Khan, Mongolian tents, and archaeological investigation of Ma'lta.

The Hermitage
http://www.hermitagemuseum.org/html_En/03/hm3_5_11.html

The Hermitage Museum provies an overview of its rich holdings in Central Asian art and artifacts, including pages devoted to the collection highlights.

International Dunhuang Project: The Silk Road Online
http://idp.bl.uk/

This site is an international collaboration of institutes holding the world's best Silk Road collections. The site includes a searchable database of art, artifacts, and documents; articles and newsletters on Silk Road history and research; and a categorized list of links to useful sites.

Monks and Merchants: Silk Road Treasures from Northwestern China, Gansu, and Ningxia
http://sites.asiasociety.org/arts/monksandmerchants/

This online exhibit from the Asia Society presents images of sculptures, artifacts, and documents, each with a short article.

Silk Road Seattle
http://depts.washington.edu/silkroad/index.html

A public education project sponsored by the University of Washington, this sprawling website includes illustrated articles on history, architecture, and culture, as well as annotated bibliographies, an electronic atlas, and historical documents translated into English.

The Transoxiana Pages
http://www.oxuscom.com/centasia.htm

This website includes a collection of articles and detailed chronologies by Mark Dickens, as well as a useful list of links to other general sites on Central Asia.

Acknowledgments

I would like to thank Nancy Toff of Oxford University Press and the series editors, Bonnie Smith and Anand Yang, for their patience and guidance in the preparation of this book. I would also like to acknowledge the sharp editorial eye of Karen Fein and the many technical contributions of Sonia Tycko.

For many years I have benefited from an ongoing conversation on Central Asian history with my friends and colleagues Thomas T. Allsen, Nicola Di Cosmo, and Anatoly M. Khazanov. I would also like to thank my students at Rutgers University to whom I first began to introduce the peoples and cultures of Central Asia some thirty-six years ago. It is with them in mind that this book was written. Needless to say, I alone am responsible for any errors of fact or mistakes in interpretation.

My son, Greg, has always managed to find time from his own busy scholarly activity to solve his father's computer problems and for that I am truly grateful. My wife, Sylvia Wu Golden, has been my greatest helpmate in all things and to her this book is dedicated.

Index

The
New
Oxford
World
History

CHRONOLOGICAL VOLUMES
The World from Beginnings to 4000 BCE
The World from 4000 to 1000 BCE
The World from 1000 bce to 500 CE
The World from 300 to 1000 CE
The World from 1000 to 1500
The World from 1450 to 1700
The World in the Eighteenth Century
The World in the Nineteenth Century
The World in the Twentieth Century

THEMATIC AND TOPICAL VOLUMES
The City: A World History
Democracy: A World History
Empires: A World History
The Family: A World History
Food: A World History
Race: A World History
Technology: A World History

GEOGRAPHICAL VOLUMES
Central Asia in World History
China in World History
Japan in World History
Russia in World History
The Silk Road in World History
South Africa in World History
South Asia in World History
Southeast Asia in World History
Trans-Saharan Africa in World History